Published by Warrior Publishing LLC First Edition: 2025

Printed in the United States of America ISBN: 978-1-952437-05-2

Cover Design by Sharon Grossman

**Disclaimer:** The information contained in this book is intended for
general informational purposes only and does not constitute professional
advice. The authors and publisher disclaim any liability for any errors or
omissions contained herein. Readers should consult with appropriate
professionals for specific advice regarding their particular circumstances.

# Contents

# Foreword

———————— ❧ ————————

When asked, "What is the most impactful talent management action a company can take to deliver value to stakeholders?" I often jest, "Place your lowest-performing employee in your competitor's organization and let them wreak havoc."

While humorous, this statement highlights a fundamental truth: organizations with superior talent outperform their peers. Employee attitude directly impacts customer satisfaction and, ultimately, financial performance. Top talent has options and will choose organizations that invest in their growth and well-being.

This exceptional book addresses these challenges head-on. It transcends mere platitudes and offers a research-backed, integrated framework for retaining top talent. Our research on the Organization Guidance System confirms that investing in talent drives strategic execution, customer loyalty, shareholder value, and community reputation.

The book's eight pillars provide a comprehensive framework for hiring, engaging, developing, rewarding, and retaining top talent. This taxonomy enables companies to organize disparate talent strategies into a coherent approach, fostering a talent science.

Case studies from diverse organizations illustrate the practical application of these principles. The 100 strategies offer a menu of specific actions that any business or HR leader can tailor to their organization. Any business or HR leader can look at the 8 pillars to decide where to focus, then select the specific actions that will make it happen.

More importantly, these insights can be personalized and tailored to your organization through the Retention100™. This allows you to set priorities and ensure that the approach to retaining top talent is not one size fits all.

This book is a comprehensive guide to talent advantage. It should not only be read for its comprehensive coverage, but earmarked, underlined, shared, and used to make sure that the right people stay in your organization.

Dave Ulrich, Ph.D.
Alpine, Utah

# How to Use the Book

——————✦——————

Congratulations on taking the first step towards building a high-performing and engaged workforce! Your purchase of this book includes exclusive access to the Retention100™ assessment. This online tool will provide you with a personalized evaluation of your current retention practices, highlighting strengths and areas for improvement.

### How to Access Your Retention100™ Assessment:

1. Visit our website: www.retention100.com
2. Enter your name and email address.
3. You'll be directed to the Retention100™ assessment, which you can download as a PDF and where you can answer a series of questions about your organization's retention practices.

**The Retention100™ assessment is your key to unlocking valuable insights that will help you:**

- Identify potential retention risks.
- Benchmark your organization against industry best practices.
- Develop a data-driven retention strategy.
- Build a more engaged and productive workforce.

**Take advantage of this opportunity and unlock the full potential of your retention efforts!**

# Preface

————— ⟡ —————

In today's competitive business landscape, employee retention has never been more critical. The costs associated with high turnover can be staggering, from lost productivity and decreased morale to the financial burden of recruitment and onboarding new hires. As organizations grapple with these challenges, it's imperative to seek effective solutions that can foster a more engaged and loyal workforce.

*Motivated to Stay* offers a comprehensive framework for addressing the complex issue of voluntary turnover. Based on the Retention100™ assessment, this book presents 100 actionable strategies that organizations can implement to improve retention rates and create a thriving workplace culture. These evidence-based strategies address the root causes of employee departures and offer practical solutions to improve retention, making it a valuable resource for organizations struggling with high turnover. When you understand the factors that influence employee loyalty and implement these strategies, you will create a more engaged, productive, and sustainable organization.

## What You'll Learn

- The real costs of high turnover and the impact it has on your organization's bottom line.
- The key reasons why employees leave their jobs and how to address these underlying issues.

- A step-by-step guide to implementing the Retention100™ assessment and analyzing your organization's specific retention challenges.

- 100 actionable strategies to improve retention, organized into eight key pillars that cover everything from compensation and benefits to workplace culture and employee engagement.

- Real-world examples from leading organizations that have successfully implemented these strategies to reduce turnover and create thriving workplaces.

## About the Authors

**Dr. William Rothwell** is a Distinguished Professor in the Workforce Education and Development program at Penn State University. With over 300 publications and a global reputation for his expertise, Dr. Rothwell brings a wealth of knowledge and experience to the topic of employee retention.

Connect with Dr. Rothwell:

- Website: https://www.rothwellandassociates.com

- LinkedIn: https://www.linkedin.com/in/bill-rothwell-2175b16

Newly promoted managers often struggle to transition into effective leaders, leading to high turnover and decreased productivity. **Dr. Sharon Grossman**, founder of Turnkey Retention Solutions, helps organizations address this challenge. Her proven strategies transform newly promoted managers into confident leaders, fostering engaged teams and boosting bottom-line results.

**Connect with Dr. Sharon:**

- Website: www.drsharongrossman.com
- LinkedIn: https://www.linkedin.com/in/sharongrossman

**Renata Scott, M.S.** is a doctoral student at Penn State University and 2023-24 University Distinguished Graduate Fellowship recipient, who leverages over a decade of counseling and career coaching experience to offer a fresh perspective on employee retention.

**Connect with Ms. Scott:**

- LinkedIn: https://www.linkedin.com/in/renatascott2020

By combining their expertise, the authors offer a comprehensive and practical guide to addressing employee turnover.

Take the first step towards improving your organization's retention rates by reading *Motivated to Stay.*

# INTRODUCTION

# The Retention Revolution

———— ✦✧✦ ————

In an era where talent is the ultimate currency, the ability to retain top performers has become a strategic imperative for organizations worldwide. Yet, despite the growing awareness of its importance, retention remains a persistent challenge. The cost of employee turnover is staggering, encompassing not just financial implications but also damage to morale, productivity, and brand reputation.

*Motivated to Stay* is a comprehensive guide that delves into the intricate psychology of retention, offering practical strategies to build a high-performance, high-retention culture. This book is not just a theoretical exploration; it's a practical toolkit designed to empower leaders to make informed decisions and implement effective retention initiatives.

In this book, you'll embark on a journey through the critical aspects of employee retention, guided by the eight pillars of the Retention100™ assessment tool. Each chapter offers a deep dive into a specific pillar, providing you with actionable insights and strategies to transform your organization's retention efforts.

In Chapter 1, you will uncover the psychological factors that drive employee loyalty and commitment. You'll gain insights into the complex decision-making process behind an employee's choice to stay or leave, setting the stage for the strategies discussed in subsequent chapters.

Chapter 2 covers the first of the 8 pillars, hiring right. Learn how to lay the groundwork for long-term retention from the very beginning. You'll explore strategies for aligning candidate values with organizational culture, the impact of realistic job previews, and how to use predictive analytics in your hiring process.

In Chapter 3, you'll dive into the world of data-driven decisions, the second pillar. Discover how to collect, analyze, and act on data to predict turnover risks and measure the effectiveness of your retention initiatives.

Chapter 4 explores the third pillar, the power of communication. You'll learn strategies for improving organizational transparency, facilitating two-way feedback, and leveraging technology to enhance communication in remote and hybrid work environments.

In Chapter 5, you'll uncover the science behind effective recognition programs, the fourth pillar. Gain insights into designing recognition initiatives that resonate with different employee demographics and align with your organizational values.

Chapter 6 delves into the fifth pillar, using reward and benefit programs. Learn how to design competitive and personalized reward systems that cater to diverse employee needs and how to communicate their value effectively.

In Chapter 7, you'll discover how investing in employee growth, the sixth pillar, can significantly boost retention rates. Explore strategies for creating personalized development plans, fostering a culture of continuous learning, and measuring the return on investment of your learning and development initiatives.

Chapter 8 focuses on the seventh pillar, building positive relationships. Learn the art of cultivating a workplace where employees feel supported and connected. Gain insights into building strong team dynamics, fostering mentorship programs, and creating an inclusive culture that enhances belonging and retention.

In Chapter 9, you'll explore the eighth pillar, onboarding and exit strategies. Discover strategies for creating impactful onboarding experiences that set new hires up for long-term success, as well as how to conduct meaningful exit interviews that provide valuable insights for improving retention.

The Epilogue will give you a glimpse into the evolving landscape of employee retention. You'll explore emerging trends, technologies, and strategies that will shape the future of talent retention.

## Throughout each chapter, you'll find:

- Compelling case studies that bring retention strategies to life
- Scientific research that underpins each pillar of the Retention100™
- Detailed explanations of how each pillar relates to the Retention100™
- Eye-opening statistics on the cost of neglecting each retention factor
- Clear illustrations of the benefits of investing in each pillar
- Practical strategies for improvement, each accompanied by a real-world example
- Honest discussions of the challenges you might face and how to overcome them

By the end of this book, you'll have a comprehensive understanding of the Retention100™ framework and a robust toolkit of strategies to dramatically improve your organization's ability to retain top talent. Whether you're a seasoned HR professional or a business leader looking to build a more stable and engaged workforce, *Motivated to Stay* will equip you with the knowledge and tools you need to succeed in the retention revolution.

# CHAPTER 1

# The Psychology of Retention: Why People Stay or Go

Imagine this: You've invested months training a promising new employee, only to watch them walk out the door after just six months. Sound familiar? You're not alone. In 2021, a staggering 47% of U.S. jobs experienced some form of employee turnover, according to the U.S. Bureau of Labor Statistics. That's nearly half of all positions! Employee turnover isn't just a minor inconvenience—it's a constant battle that drains your finances, erodes morale, and hinders your ability to grow.

In this chapter, we'll explore the critical importance of retention and its impact on your organization's success. We'll delve into the reasons behind the rising turnover rates and the cost implications for businesses today. You'll discover effective strategies to foster a culture of retention, including leadership's role in shaping a supportive environment, the value of professional development, and the power of recognition and flexibility.

Additionally, we'll discuss how to create a sense of purpose and belonging within your team. As we journey through this chapter and the rest of the book, you'll gain the insights and tools needed to not only reduce turnover but to transform your organization into a thriving workplace where employees feel valued and motivated to stay.

## Why Retention Matters Now More Than Ever

Employee retention has emerged as a critical issue for organizations across all industries. With shifting workforce demographics, increasing mobility, and rising employee expectations, retaining top talent is no longer just a strategic priority—it's a competitive necessity. High turnover costs extend beyond financial losses; they impact organizational culture, productivity, and customer satisfaction.

To better understand the importance of retention, it's essential to define key terms. **Turnover** refers to the rate at which employees leave an organization and can be calculated using the formula:

$$\left( \frac{\text{Total number of employees who left}}{(\text{Employees you started with} + \text{Employees you ended up with}) / 2} \right) \times 100 = \text{Turnover Rate}$$

In contrast, **retention** measures the percentage of employees who remain with the organization over a specific period. The retention rate can be calculated as follows:

$$\left( \frac{\text{Total number of current employees}}{\text{Total number of original employees}} \right) \times 100 = \text{Retention Rate}$$

Employee turnover imposes substantial costs on organizations, encompassing both direct expenses and hidden impacts. The cost of replacing an employee can vary depending on factors such as the position's seniority and the company's size. However, as of 2023, the average cost of replacing an employee in the U.S. is $4,700. This figure includes expenses related to recruitment, onboarding, training, and lost productivity.

To calculate the cost per hire, consider factors such as advertising costs, recruiter fees, background checks, and onboarding expenses. The cost of lost productivity includes the time spent on training new employees, reduced output during the onboarding period, and the potential impact on team morale and customer satisfaction.

As we explore the changing landscape of work and its implications for retention strategies, it becomes clear that fostering a positive work environment and investing in employee development are essential for mitigating turnover costs and building a stable workforce.

But here's the good news: by understanding the changing nature of work and implementing effective retention strategies, you can create a culture where employees are motivated to stay, grow, and contribute.

## The Changing Landscape of Work

The nature of work has undergone a significant transformation in recent years, driven by technological advancements, shifting demographics, and evolving societal expectations. This new landscape presents both challenges and opportunities for employee retention.

## Remote and Hybrid Work Models

The rise of remote and hybrid work has redefined the traditional workplace. While offering unprecedented flexibility, it also challenges organizations to maintain strong workplace cultures and employee connections across distributed teams. This shift has expanded the talent pool but intensified competition for skilled workers, as geographic boundaries no longer limit job opportunities.

## The Gig Economy

The growing gig economy offers workers autonomy and flexibility but poses retention challenges for organizations. Companies must now consider how to build loyalty and engagement among a more transient workforce.

## Demographic and Generational Shifts

Younger generations, particularly Millennials and Gen Z, bring different values and expectations to the workplace. They prioritize purpose-driven work, work-life balance, and professional development over traditional job security. Organizations must adapt their retention strategies to cater to these changing values.

## Technology's Evolving Role

Advancements in AI, machine learning, and automation are reshaping job roles. Employees now seek opportunities to apply uniquely human skills like creativity and critical thinking. Organizations that provide meaningful work and invest in employee development are more likely to retain top talent.

## Shifting Employee Expectations

Today's workforce expects more from their employers, including alignment with personal values, transparency, and a focus on well-being. Organizations must prioritize these aspects to build a reputation as a desirable place to work.

## The Retention Imperative

Retention strategies need to evolve beyond competitive salaries and benefits. The changing landscape we've explored demands a more holistic approach to keeping your best talent engaged and committed. It's time to shift your focus from simply preventing employees from leaving to creating an environment where they actively want to stay, grow, and contribute.

To build a culture of retention, start with your leadership. Remember, leaders set the tone for the entire organization. They influence how employees perceive their roles and the overall work environment. When leaders model behaviors that prioritize employee well-being, open communication, and inclusivity, they create a supportive atmosphere where employees feel valued and engaged. This isn't just about recognizing individual contributions—it's about fostering a culture of collaboration and trust.

As we move forward in this book, we'll explore actionable strategies to help you cultivate this culture within your organization. Get ready to transform retention from a challenge into a powerful driver of your business success.

## The Real Costs of Losing Employees

Sarah, a brilliant software engineer, just left Acme Tech after three years on the job. Her departure isn't just a blip on the HR radar—it's a seismic event that's going to ripple through the entire company for months to come.

First off, let's talk money. Replacing Sarah isn't going to be cheap. Estimates suggest that replacing an employee can cost between 16% and 20% of their annual salary, and we're looking at potentially twice her salary when you factor in all the costs. There's the $4,000 job ad, the countless hours of interviews (goodbye, productivity!), and the whole onboarding process. According to the Society for Human Resource Management (SHRM), the average cost per hire rose to $4,700 in 2023.

Job Ad Posted → Interviews → Onboarding → 3 Months at 75% Productivity

## To calculate the exact cost of losing Sarah, we can use the following formula:

Cost of Turnover = (Cost per Hire + Cost of Lost Productivity) x Number of Departures

Assuming Sarah's annual salary was $100,000, the cost of replacing her would be:

- Cost per Hire: $4,700
- Cost of Lost Productivity: Assuming a 3-month ramp-up period and a 25% reduction in productivity during that time, the cost would be approximately $25,000 (3 months x 25% x $100,000).

**Total Cost of Turnover:** ($4,700 + $25,000) x 1 = $29,700

But here's the kicker—the real cost goes way beyond the numbers on a spreadsheet. Sarah's team is in shambles. They were in the middle of a major project, and now they're scrambling to pick up the pieces. Morale? It's taken a nosedive. The remaining team members are looking at each other, wondering, "Who's next?" And you can bet they're updating their resumes as we speak.

Now, the new hire? Sure, they might be great, but they're not Sarah. For the next three months, they'll be about 25% less productive as they learn the ropes. That's a quarter of their potential just... poof! Gone. All that institutional knowledge Sarah had? That's walked out the door with her. You can't put a price tag on three years of experience and relationships.

And don't even get us started on how this looks to the outside world. Potential candidates are going to think twice before applying to a company with a reputation for high turnover. Clients? They're not thrilled about having to build relationships with a new account manager every six months. A study highlighted that in 2019, employee turnover cost U.S. industries over $630 billion. Furthermore, the cost of talent shortages is projected to reach $435.7 billion for the U.S., $90 billion for the United Kingdom, and $147.1 billion for China.

So, when we talk about the cost of losing an employee like Sarah, we're not just talking about a line item in the budget. We're talking about a complex web of financial, cultural, and reputational impacts that can take years to fully recover from. Given these considerable expenses—both monetary and otherwise—it is imperative for organizations to implement effective retention strategies.

Is turnover silently draining your company's resources? Discover the hidden costs with our **Turnover Cost Calculator,** available at www.drsharongrossman.com/calculator.

Input your organization's specific data to uncover the true financial impact of employee turnover. Take the first step towards a more cost-effective and efficient workforce.

## Why Do Employees Leave? Getting to the Heart of the Issue

Sarah's departure wasn't just a random event—it's a symptom of deeper issues that many companies face. Understanding why Sarah left is like solving a puzzle, and each piece gives us insight into how we can prevent similar departures in the future.

So, why did Sarah leave? Well, it could be a mix of things. Maybe she felt like a small cog in a big machine, her innovative ideas getting lost in the bureaucratic shuffle. Or perhaps she was lured away by a competitor offering a juicier salary package and the promise of leading her own team. It's also possible that Sarah was burning the midnight oil too often, her work-life balance tipping dangerously towards all work and no play.

But here's the thing—Sarah's departure wasn't inevitable. It falls into what we call "avoidable turnover." That's the kind of turnover that keeps HR managers up at night because, with the right strategies, it could have been prevented.

Let's break it down. Maybe Sarah felt her career was stagnating. In a fast-paced field like software engineering, if you're not moving forward, you're falling behind. If Acme Tech didn't have a clear path for Sarah's growth or wasn't investing in her skill development, it's no wonder she started looking elsewhere.

Or it could be about recognition. Did anyone at Acme Tech notice when Sarah pulled an all-nighter to fix that critical bug? Did they celebrate when her innovative feature boosted user engagement by 20%? Sometimes, a simple "great job" can be the difference between an employee who's engaged and one who's updating their LinkedIn profile.

Then there's the culture piece. Tech companies often pride themselves on their cool, collaborative cultures. But if Sarah felt isolated, if she didn't click with her team or felt her ideas were being dismissed, that's a recipe for disengagement. And disengaged employees are as good as gone.

Of course, we can't rule out the possibility that Sarah's departure was due to something outside of Acme Tech's control. Maybe her partner got a dream job in another city, or she decided to take a year off to travel the world. That would fall under "unavoidable turnover"—the kind that happens no matter how great your retention strategies are.

The key here is to figure out which category Sarah's departure falls into. If it's avoidable, that's your cue to dig deeper and make changes. Maybe it's time to revamp your professional development programs, or take a hard look at your company culture. If it's unavoidable, well, that's life—but it's still an opportunity to learn and improve your offboarding process.

Understanding why employees like Sarah leave isn't just about plugging holes in a leaky ship. It's about creating an environment where your best people want to stay, grow, and thrive. It's about building a workplace that's not just a pit stop in someone's career, but a destination. And that is the secret sauce of successful companies.

## Building a Culture of Retention

Cultivating a culture of retention is essential for organizations aiming to thrive. Employee retention has become one of the most pressing challenges across all industries, driven by shifting workforce demographics, increasing mobility, and rising expectations. High turnover rates not only incur substantial financial costs, but also disrupt organizational culture, productivity, and customer satisfaction. As you navigate this landscape, it's crucial to understand why retention matters now more than ever and how you can implement effective strategies to foster a supportive work environment.

Effective leadership is fundamental to establishing a retention-focused culture. As a leader, you set the tone for your workplace, creating an atmosphere where employees feel respected and appreciated. It's about embodying your organization's values and serving as a role model. When employees see you demonstrate respect, inclusivity, and empathy, they are more likely to mirror those behaviors, fostering a sense of belonging.

Open communication is equally vital; being approachable encourages employees to voice their concerns and ideas without fear. This creates a psychologically safe environment where they feel valued. Regular feedback—both constructive and recognition of achievements—keeps employees engaged and committed.

Investing in professional development is one of the most effective retention strategies available. Employees want to advance their careers, and organizations that prioritize their growth are more likely to retain top talent. This investment can take many forms—training programs, mentorship opportunities, or access to conferences—and shows your commitment to their long-term success. Encouraging continuous learning through knowledge sharing and collaboration significantly impacts retention as well; when employees feel empowered to explore new ideas and work together, they become more invested in the organization's success.

Recognition also plays a critical role in building a culture of retention. Employees who feel acknowledged are more likely to remain loyal. Recognition should go beyond formal reward programs; it should include genuine thanks for both big and small contributions.

Flexibility in the workplace has emerged as another key driver of retention. Options for remote work or flexible hours are increasingly important as employees prioritize work-life balance. Organizations that support this balance demonstrate a commitment to employee well-being, which builds loyalty and trust.

As you work to create a culture of retention, remember that fostering purpose and belonging is essential. Connect employees to your organization's mission and values, showing them how their roles contribute to larger goals. When employees see their work as meaningful, they are more likely to stay committed. Building a sense of belonging involves embracing diversity and celebrating inclusivity through team-building activities and mentorship programs.

Ultimately, fostering retention isn't just about keeping employees happy; it's about securing your organization's long-term success. The costs associated with turnover—like recruitment expenses and lost productivity—can significantly impact your bottom line. By investing in retention strategies that prioritize employee well-being, development, recognition, flexibility, and purpose, you can create a supportive environment that attracts top talent and fosters loyalty.

As you embark on this journey toward building a culture of retention, remember that it requires ongoing effort and commitment from everyone in the organization. By prioritizing these elements, you can create an engaged workforce that not only stays but thrives—ultimately driving your organization toward greater success in an increasingly competitive market.

## Your Roadmap to Retention

This book is designed specifically for leaders and HR professionals who are tired of the revolving door.

**Here's what you can expect:**

- **Uncover the hidden costs of turnover:** We'll go beyond the financial burden to explore the impact on your company culture, brand image, and overall success.

- **Understand why employees leave:** We'll delve into the root causes of turnover, differentiating between voluntary (employee-initiated) and involuntary (employer-initiated) departures.

- **Identify areas for improvement:** We'll introduce the Retention100™, a powerful tool to help you diagnose your specific retention challenges.

- **Develop targeted strategies:** Using the insights from the Retention100™, you'll learn actionable steps to create a work environment that fosters loyalty and engagement, keeping your top talent on board.

By the end of this book, you'll be equipped to not only understand why employees leave, but also take proactive measures to stop the revolving door and build a thriving workforce.

## About the Retention100™

Let's talk about your new secret weapon in the fight against turnover - the Retention100™. This isn't just another HR buzzword or a fancy chart to hang on your office wall. It's a comprehensive, actionable framework that's going to revolutionize how you think about and tackle employee retention.

The Retention100™ breaks down the complex challenge of retention into eight key pillars. Think of these pillars as the load-bearing walls of your retention strategy. If one of them is weak, the whole structure is at risk of collapsing.

## Here's the rundown:

1. **Hiring Right**: This is all about building a solid foundation. We're talking about finding the right people who not only have the skills but also fit your company culture. It's like

dating - you want to make sure there's a good match before you commit.

2. **Data-Driven Decisions**: In today's world, gut feelings aren't enough. This pillar is about using cold, hard data to inform your retention strategies. We're talking performance metrics, absenteeism rates - the works. It's like having a crystal ball, but better because it's based on facts.

3. **The Power of Communication**: This pillar is all about keeping your employees in the loop and feeling valued. It's about creating a culture of trust, empowerment, and purpose. Think of it as the WD-40 of your organization - it keeps everything running smoothly.

4. **Recognizing Achievements**: Everyone likes a pat on the back now and then. This pillar focuses on making sure your employees feel appreciated. It's amazing how far a simple "great job" can go in keeping someone motivated.

5. **Offering Rewards:** This goes hand in hand with recognition. It's about putting your money where your mouth is and investing in your people. Remember, a happy employee is a loyal employee.

6. **Learning and Development**: People want to grow, both personally and professionally. This pillar is about providing those opportunities through training, mentorship, and coaching. It's like watering a plant - nurture it, and it'll flourish.

7. **Building Positive Relationships**: No one wants to work in a toxic environment. This pillar focuses on fostering a

supportive workplace where people actually want to come to work every day.

8.  **Onboarding and Exit Strategies:** First impressions matter, and so do last ones. This pillar covers everything from smooth onboarding to constructive exit interviews. It's about making sure every interaction with your company is a positive one.

Now, here's the cool part. The Retention100™ isn't just a list of best practices. It's a diagnostic tool that helps you identify where your retention strategy might be falling short. It's like a health check-up for your organization.

By assessing your company against these eight pillars, you'll get a clear picture of where you're nailing it and where you need to up your game. And the best part? Once you've identified your weak spots, this book will give you concrete strategies to strengthen them.

So, are you ready to turn your company into a place where people want to stay and grow? The Retention100™ is your roadmap. Let's get started!

### Your Retention Action Plan

We recommend that you form a team of 7-12 people from different levels of the organization to fill out the Retention100™ online. Based on your results, create a tailored action plan that addresses the most critical areas for improvement. Consider the following steps:

1.  **Prioritize Areas of Focus:** Identify the 3-5 most pressing retention challenges highlighted in your assessment. These

might include issues related to compensation, work-life balance, career development, or management practices.

2. **Select Targeted Strategies**: From the extensive list of action strategies provided in the Retention100™, choose those that directly address your prioritized areas of focus. Consider your organization's specific needs, resources, and culture when making your selections.

3. **Develop Actionable Steps**: For each selected strategy, outline specific, measurable actions that you will take to implement it. Define clear objectives, timelines, and responsible parties.

4. **Allocate Resources**: Determine the necessary resources, including budget, personnel, and time, to support the implementation of your action plan.

5. **Track Progress and Measure Outcomes**: Establish metrics to monitor the progress of your retention initiatives. Regularly track key performance indicators (KPIs) such as turnover rates, employee satisfaction scores, and absenteeism rates.

**List your organization's scores below:**

| Retention Pillar | Items on the Retention100™ | Total items utilized by your organization | Check if this is an area you will focus on |
|---|---|---|---|
| Hiring Right | 1-6 | /6 | |
| Data-Driven Decisions | 7-18 | /12 | |
| Communication | 19-32 | /14 | |

| | | | |
|---|---|---|---|
| Recognizing Achievements | 33-37 | /5 | |
| Using Reward and Benefit Programs | 38-61 | /24 | |
| Learning & Development | 62-73 | /12 | |
| Positive Relationships | 74-98 | /25 | |
| Onboarding & Exit Strategies | 99-100 | /2 | |

## Our 3-5 selected action items:

1._____

2. _____

3. _____

4. _____

5. _____

# CHAPTER 2

# Pillar 1 - Hiring Right: Building a Foundation for Retention

———— ❧ ————

So, you want to build a workplace where people love to come to work every day? Well, the first step is *hiring right.* It's like building a house – if the foundation is shaky, the whole thing is gonna crumble. Hiring the right people isn't just about filling positions; it's about finding folks who fit in like a glove. They need to align with your company's values, culture, and long-term goals.

When you nail the hiring process, it's like a domino effect. The right people make better decisions, communicate more effectively, and feel more connected to the company.

They're more motivated by rewards and recognition, and they're more likely to take advantage of learning and development opportunities. Plus, they create a positive work environment where everyone feels supported and valued. Basically, hiring right is the cornerstone of employee retention. It sets the stage for everything else, from communication to rewards to development.

## Case Study: The Downfall of Crestwood Manufacturing

Crestwood Manufacturing, a fast-growing furniture company, made a big mistake. They hired 50 new people in a hurry and didn't take the time to do it right. They skipped background checks, rushed interviews, and didn't even bother to see if the new folks were a good fit for the company.

It was a disaster. The new hires didn't know what they were doing, they didn't care about the company, and they didn't stick around. Crestwood lost a ton of money and had to deal with a bunch of unhappy customers. It's a clear lesson: don't rush the hiring process. Take your time, find the right people, and build a strong foundation for your company.

## The Science Behind Effective Hiring

Ever wondered why some companies seem to have a magic touch when it comes to keeping their employees around? It's not just about fancy perks or ping pong tables. It's about hiring the *right* people.

You see, the science of effective hiring is grounded in psychology and behavior. When you get it right, it's like building a house on a solid foundation. The whole thing is stronger, more stable, and less likely to crumble.

One of the biggest secrets is finding the perfect match. Think about it: when you find a job that fits like a glove, you're more likely to love it, right? It's the same for your employees. When their skills, values, and personalities align with the company's culture and the job itself, they're happier, more engaged, and way less likely to quit. Research shows that this "person-job fit" can reduce turnover by a whopping 23%!

Another magic ingredient is expectations. When employees know exactly what to expect, they're less likely to get surprised or disappointed.

Onboarding is like welcoming a new family member. When you make them feel welcome and part of the team from the very beginning, they're more likely to stick around. Studies show that effective onboarding can boost retention by 82% and productivity by over 70%. Imagine that!

And let's not forget about the cost of losing people. Replacing an employee can be a major hit to your wallet. Some studies say it can cost up to 200% of their annual salary! So, by hiring the right people and keeping them around, you're not just saving money, you're also building a stronger, more stable company.

In short, the science of effective hiring is all about creating a winning team. When you find the right people, give them clear expectations, and make them feel welcome, you're setting yourself up for success. It's like building a championship team – you need the right players to win the game.

## The Cost of Hiring Wrong: A Recipe for Disaster

Ever heard the saying, "You get what you pay for?" Well, it's true in the world of hiring. When you cut corners and hire the wrong people, you're setting yourself up for a whole lot of trouble.

First off, it's a productivity killer. Imagine a team where everyone is pulling in different directions. When you hire people who don't fit the job or the company culture, they're less motivated, less engaged, and less productive. In fact, disengaged employees can be up to 18% less productive than their happy, engaged coworkers.

But the damage doesn't stop there. When you hire the wrong people, it can create a toxic work environment. Imagine working with someone who's always complaining or who doesn't care about their job. It can bring down morale and make everyone else miserable. Studies show that companies with high turnover rates often have lower job growth and a decline in their stock price.

So, what's the bottom line? Hiring the right people is essential for the long-term success of your organization. It's not just about filling positions; it's about building a strong team that can help you achieve your goals. When you invest in hiring the right people, you're investing in the future of your company.

## The Benefits of Improved Hiring

Effective hiring practices are foundational to building a thriving organization. When managed well, these practices lead to positive outcomes for both employees and the organization, including improved engagement, satisfaction, and loyalty.

Here are some key benefits:

## Employee Engagement

When companies hire the right people for the right roles, it leads to higher employee engagement. Engaged employees are not only more productive but also contribute to better business outcomes. For instance, a Gallup study found that companies with highly engaged teams are 21% more profitable. Engaged employees tend to be more committed, put in extra effort, and take ownership of their work. Plus, they're less likely to be absent—Gallup noted that engaged teams see 41% lower absenteeism, which keeps projects on track and eases the load on their colleagues.

## Employee Satisfaction

Hiring employees who fit their skills and interests significantly boosts job satisfaction. Happy employees are more likely to stick around long-term. Research shows that high satisfaction can lead to a 50% increase in loyalty and a 37% boost in retention rates. When organizations focus on cultural fit during hiring, they create a positive workplace where employees feel valued. In fact, 88% of HR professionals believe a strong company culture is crucial for success.

## A Positive Reputation

Companies that excel in hiring develop strong reputations as great places to work, attracting top talent. According to LinkedIn, 75% of job seekers consider an employer's brand before applying. A solid employer brand not only draws in quality candidates but also gives companies a competitive edge. Take Google, for example; its rigorous hiring process and employee-centric culture help maintain high retention rates while driving innovation.

## The Retention100™: How to Hire Hiring the Right People

Pillar 1 (items 1–6) of the Retention100™ delves into your organization's recruitment and selection procedures, examining how effectively they contribute to long-term employee retention. It encourages you to:

- **Assess stability:** Review each job applicant's work history to identify patterns of job hopping or frequent changes in employment. This can provide insights into the applicant's commitment level and potential for long-term retention.

- **Showcase your commitment to longevity:** Explain to prospective employees how the organization celebrates long service through employee recognition initiatives. This demonstrates the value placed on employee tenure and creates a sense of belonging and loyalty.

- **Understand candidate expectations:** Include a question on job applications that directly asks about the applicant's expectations regarding long-term employment. This information can help identify candidates who are aligned with the organization's commitment to longevity.

- **Reward employee referrals:** Recognize and reward long-serving staff members who recommend potential hires who are likely to become long-term employees. This fosters a culture of employee advocacy and encourages existing employees to contribute to the organization's talent acquisition efforts.

Carefully evaluating these aspects of your recruitment and selection procedures allows you to identify areas for improvement and implement strategies that attract and retain employees committed to the organization's long-term success.

## Strategies for Hiring Right

1. Define Clear Job Roles and Expectations

2. Focus on Cultural Fit

3. Implement Structured and Multi-Stage Interviews

4. Leverage Data-Driven Hiring Tools

5. Prioritize Diversity and Inclusion

6. Enhance Onboarding and Socialization

7. Engage in Continuous Feedback and Development

8. Build a Strong Employer Brand

9. Offer Competitive Compensation and Benefits

10. Regularly Review and Improve Hiring Practices

## Strategy 1: Define Clear Job Roles and Expectations

The strategy for improving hiring practices begins with developing detailed job descriptions and clearly communicating expectations during the hiring process. Job descriptions should be specific, outlining key responsibilities, required skills, and performance expectations. During interviews, it is essential to thoroughly discuss these aspects to ensure that candidates fully understand what the role entails and how it aligns with the organization's needs. When applying situational leadership principles, the level of detail in job descriptions and discussions should be adapted based on the candidate's experience. For less experienced candidates, offering more structured guidance is beneficial, while seasoned professionals can be given greater autonomy in their roles.

## Real-World Example: Siemens

Siemens, a global technology company, effectively implements the strategy of defining clear job roles and expectations through its comprehensive hiring and onboarding processes. Recognizing the importance of clarity in roles, Siemens develops detailed job descriptions that outline specific responsibilities, required skills, and performance metrics for each position. This ensures that candidates understand exactly what is expected of them and how their roles contribute to the company's broader objectives.

During the interview process, Siemens emphasizes thorough discussions around these job descriptions. Interviewers engage candidates in conversations about their understanding of the role and how they envision their contributions to the team. This approach not only clarifies expectations but also allows candidates to assess their fit within the organization. For less experienced candidates, Siemens provides structured guidance on key responsibilities, while seasoned professionals are encouraged to discuss their strategic vision for the role, reflecting situational leadership principles.

Furthermore, Siemens regularly reviews and updates job descriptions to align with evolving business needs and market conditions. This commitment to clarity helps foster a culture of accountability and high performance, as employees are well-informed about their duties and how success is measured. By prioritizing clear role definitions, Siemens enhances employee engagement and retention while driving organizational success.

## Strategy 2: Focus on Cultural Fit

The strategy for assessing candidates focuses on evaluating their alignment with the organization's culture and values. This can be implemented by using behavioral interview questions and cultural assessments to determine how well candidates match the organization's core values and work environment. Including team members in the interview process helps ensure the candidate fits well with the existing team dynamics. When applying transformational leadership principles, candidates should be encouraged to share their vision and explain how they see themselves contributing to the company's mission, fostering a shared sense of purpose within the organization.

## Real-World Example: Airbnb

Airbnb exemplifies Strategy 2 by prioritizing cultural fit in its hiring process through the "Core Values" interview. This unique approach assesses candidates based on their alignment with Airbnb's core values: "Be a Host," "Champion the Mission," "Be a Cereal Entrepreneur," and "Embrace the Adventure."

During this interview, candidates answer behavioral questions that reveal how they embody these values. For instance, to assess "Be a Host," candidates might share experiences where they went above and beyond to help others. Team members from various departments participate in the interview process, ensuring a well-rounded assessment of the candidate's fit within the company culture.

Additionally, candidates are encouraged to express their vision for their role and how they can contribute to Airbnb's mission. This strategy helps identify individuals who are not only skilled but also passionate about the company's purpose.

As a result, Airbnb has cultivated a strong, cohesive culture that supports its rapid growth and success, leading to higher employee engagement and lower turnover rates compared to industry averages.

## Strategy 3: Implement Structured and Multi-Stage Interviews

The strategy for thoroughly evaluating candidates involves using a structured interview process with multiple stages. This begins with a phone screening to assess basic qualifications, followed by more in-depth in-person or virtual interviews that focus on evaluating technical skills, cultural fit, and situational judgment. Incorporating assessments or work samples that are relevant to the role further enhances the evaluation process. For task-oriented leadership, the emphasis should be on the candidate's ability to meet specific job requirements and deliver on key performance indicators (KPIs). Competency-based interview techniques are effective in focusing on these critical aspects of the candidate's potential performance.

## Real-World Example: Procter & Gamble

Procter & Gamble's (P&G) "Success Drivers" assessment is a shining example of how to implement structured and multi-stage interviews effectively. This global consumer goods giant has developed a comprehensive process that goes far beyond the typical resume review and single interview. P&G's approach is designed to thoroughly evaluate candidates across various dimensions, ensuring they find the best fit for both the role and the company culture.

The process kicks off with an online application and a series of assessments, including cognitive ability and situational judgment tests. This initial screening helps P&G identify candidates with the problem-solving skills and cultural alignment they're looking for.

From there, successful applicants move on to a virtual job preview, giving them a taste of what the role entails and allowing for self-assessment. The journey continues with multiple rounds of structured interviews, each focusing on P&G's core competencies or "Success Drivers," such as leadership, innovation, and collaboration. Throughout these interviews, candidates are asked to provide specific examples of how they've demonstrated key skills in past experiences, aligning with task-oriented leadership principles.

The final stages of P&G's hiring process include a job-specific task or case study and a panel interview with senior leaders. This thorough approach has paid off handsomely for P&G. The company consistently ranks as a top employer, boasting high retention rates and strong performance from new hires. By giving candidates a clear understanding of P&G's culture and expectations throughout the process, the company sets the stage for better job satisfaction and performance once hired. It's a testament to the power of structured, multi-stage interviews in building a foundation for long-term employee retention and success.

## Strategy 4: Leverage Data-Driven Hiring Tools

The strategy to enhance decision-making in hiring involves the use of data-driven tools and assessments. This can be implemented by incorporating pre-employment assessments, such as cognitive ability tests, personality assessments, and job simulations, to gather objective data on a candidate's suitability for the role. Additionally, analyzing historical data can help identify hiring patterns that contribute to long-term retention. For analytical leadership, the decision-making process should emphasize data by setting up dashboards to track candidate performance metrics throughout the hiring process, ensuring a more informed and accurate selection.

## Real-World Example: Unilever

Unilever, the global consumer goods giant, exemplifies the strategy of leveraging data-driven hiring tools through its innovative digital recruitment process. In 2016, the company completely overhauled its traditional hiring methods, implementing a comprehensive data-driven approach to attract and assess early career talent.

The new process begins with candidates playing neuroscience-based games to evaluate their aptitude, followed by video interviews analyzed by AI algorithms. These tools assess candidates on various attributes, including problem-solving skills, communication abilities, and personality traits that align with Unilever's values. The company also utilizes job simulations that replicate real work scenarios, providing objective data on how candidates might perform in the actual role.

To support analytical leadership, Unilever developed a sophisticated dashboard that tracks candidate performance metrics throughout the hiring process. This allows hiring managers to make more informed decisions based on objective data rather than subjective impressions. The dashboard also helps identify patterns in successful hires, which informs future recruitment strategies and contributes to long-term retention efforts.

As a result of this data-driven approach, Unilever has seen remarkable improvements in its hiring outcomes. The company reports a significant increase in the diversity of its candidate pool, a 50% reduction in time-to-hire, and a notable improvement in the quality of hires. Additionally, candidate satisfaction with the recruitment process has increased, with many applicants praising the fairness and transparency of the data-driven method.

## Strategy 5: Prioritize Diversity and Inclusion

The strategy to promote diversity and inclusion in hiring focuses on creating a more dynamic and innovative workforce. This can be achieved by expanding recruiting efforts to reach diverse talent pools, using blind resume reviews to minimize bias, and assembling diverse interview panels. Additionally, crafting inclusive job descriptions that appeal to a broad audience ensures the organization attracts a wide range of candidates. For inclusive leadership, it is important to foster an environment where diverse perspectives are valued and to demonstrate a strong commitment to equity in both hiring practices and career advancement opportunities.

## Real-World Example: Accenture

Accenture, a global professional services company, has made significant strides in prioritizing diversity and inclusion through its comprehensive "Inclusion & Diversity" initiative. This program exemplifies the strategy of promoting diversity and inclusion in hiring, with remarkable results that have transformed the company's workforce and culture.

At the heart of Accenture's approach is a multi-faceted recruitment strategy. The company has expanded its talent sourcing efforts by partnering with diverse professional organizations, historically black colleges and universities (HBCUs), and women's colleges. They've also implemented blind resume reviews, removing identifying information such as names and addresses to minimize unconscious bias in the initial screening process. Furthermore, Accenture ensures that interview panels are diverse, representing various backgrounds, genders, and ethnicities to provide a more inclusive candidate experience.

The impact of these efforts has been substantial. Accenture has seen a significant increase in the diversity of its workforce, with women now comprising 45% of their global workforce and 25% of managing directors. The company has also achieved gender parity in promotions, hiring, and retention. Moreover, Accenture reports that this focus on diversity and inclusion has led to increased innovation, with diverse teams generating more creative solutions for clients. As a result, Accenture has been recognized as a leader in workplace diversity, consistently ranking high on various diversity indices and attracting top talent from underrepresented groups.

## Strategy 6: Enhance Onboarding and Socialization

The strategy of investing in a comprehensive onboarding process aims to effectively integrate new hires into the organization. This can be implemented by developing a structured onboarding program that includes orientation, training, and mentorship. Each new hire should be paired with a buddy or mentor who can guide them through their first few months, helping them assimilate into the company culture. For coaching leadership, the emphasis is on creating personalized onboarding experiences that address the unique needs of each individual, offering continuous feedback to support their development and ensure their success within the organization.

## Real-World Example: IBM

IBM, the multinational technology corporation, has implemented a comprehensive onboarding strategy called the "New IBMer" program to effectively integrate new hires into their organization. This program exemplifies Strategy 6 by providing a structured approach to orientation, training, and mentorship for all new employees.

The "New IBMer" program begins with a personalized digital welcome experience that introduces new hires to IBM's culture, values, and global operations. This is followed by a series of in-person and virtual training sessions that cover essential skills and knowledge specific to their roles. A key component of the program is the assignment of a "buddy" to each new hire - an experienced IBM employee who serves as a mentor and guide during the first few months of employment. This buddy system helps newcomers navigate the company's complex structure and culture, providing invaluable support and insights.

IBM's approach to onboarding also emphasizes continuous feedback and personalized development. New hires participate in regular check-ins with their managers and HR representatives to discuss their progress, address any challenges, and set goals for their future at the company. This coaching-focused approach ensures that each employee receives tailored support to meet their unique needs and aspirations. As a result of this comprehensive onboarding strategy, IBM has reported improved employee engagement, faster time-to-productivity for new hires, and higher retention rates among recent joiners.

## Strategy 7: Engage in Continuous Feedback and Development

The strategy to establish a culture of continuous feedback and professional development focuses on fostering employee growth and satisfaction from the start. This can be implemented by conducting regular check-ins during the initial months of employment to assess new hires' satisfaction and address any concerns early. Offering opportunities for skill development and career advancement further demonstrates the organization's commitment to their growth. For servant leadership, the priority is on the development and well-being of new hires, actively seeking their feedback and supporting their career progression to ensure they feel valued and empowered in their roles.

## Real-World Example: Spotify

Spotify, the global music streaming platform, exemplifies Strategy 7 through its innovative "Amplify" program, which focuses on continuous feedback and development for employees. This initiative demonstrates Spotify's commitment to fostering a culture of growth and open communication from the moment new hires join the company.

The "Amplify" program begins with bi-weekly check-ins between new employees and their managers during the first three months of employment. These sessions are designed to assess the new hire's integration into the team, address any concerns, and provide timely support. As part of this process, Spotify uses a digital feedback tool that allows employees to share their thoughts and experiences in real-time, ensuring that potential issues are identified and addressed promptly. This approach aligns with servant leadership principles, as managers actively seek feedback and prioritize the well-being of their team members.

Beyond the initial onboarding period, Spotify continues to invest in its employees' growth through various development initiatives. The company offers a personalized learning and development platform called "GreenHouse," which provides access to a wide range of courses, workshops, and mentoring opportunities. Employees are encouraged to dedicate time each week to their professional development, with managers playing a supportive role in helping team members identify areas for growth and create tailored development plans. This commitment to ongoing learning and career progression has contributed to Spotify's high employee satisfaction rates and its reputation as an employer of choice in the tech industry.

## Strategy 8: Build a Strong Employer Brand

The strategy to cultivate a positive employer brand aims to attract and retain top talent by showcasing the company's strengths. This can be implemented by highlighting the organization's culture, values, and employee success stories on platforms such as the company website, social media, and during interviews. It is also essential to provide candidates with a realistic preview of the company culture and work environment, ensuring transparency. For charismatic leadership, the focus is on using leadership presence to personally communicate the company's mission, values, and vision, inspiring candidates to envision themselves as part of a larger, meaningful purpose within the organization.

## Real-World Example: IKEA

IKEA, the Swedish-founded multinational furniture retailer, has successfully implemented Strategy 8 by building a strong employer brand through its "IKEA Values" campaign. This initiative showcases the company's unique culture, values, and employee experiences across various platforms, attracting top talent and fostering a sense of belonging among current employees.

At the heart of IKEA's employer branding strategy is its commitment to transparency and authenticity. The company's career website features a dedicated section called "Life at IKEA," which provides potential candidates with an honest and realistic preview of the work environment. This section includes employee testimonials, day-in-the-life videos, and detailed information about IKEA's sustainability initiatives and diversity programs. By offering this transparent look into the company culture, IKEA ensures that candidates can make informed decisions about whether they align with the organization's values and work style.

IKEA's co-founder and former CEO, Ingvar Kamprad, played a crucial role in shaping the company's employer brand through charismatic leadership. Even after stepping down from his executive role, Kamprad continued to embody IKEA's values and vision, often sharing stories and insights that inspired both employees and potential candidates. This approach has created a legacy of leadership that continues to influence IKEA's employer brand, with current leaders regularly engaging in public speaking events and media interviews to communicate the company's mission and values. As a result, IKEA has cultivated a strong employer brand that attracts candidates who are not just looking for a job, but for a meaningful career aligned with their personal values and aspirations.

## Strategy 9: Offer Competitive Compensation and Benefits

The strategy of offering a compensation and benefits package that meets or exceeds industry standards is essential for attracting and retaining top talent. This can be implemented by regularly conducting market research to ensure the company's offerings remain competitive. The package should include not only salary but also comprehensive benefits such as health insurance, retirement plans, flexible working arrangements, and opportunities for professional development. For visionary leadership, it's important to connect compensation and benefits to the long-term vision of the company, demonstrating to candidates how their roles and rewards will evolve as the organization achieves its strategic goals, fostering a sense of shared growth and future potential.

## Real-World Example: Netflix

Netflix, the global streaming giant, has implemented a unique and highly competitive compensation strategy that exemplifies Strategy 9. The company's approach to compensation and benefits goes beyond traditional models, focusing on attracting and retaining top talent in the highly competitive tech and entertainment industries.

At the core of Netflix's compensation philosophy is the concept of "top of market" pay. The company regularly conducts market research to ensure that its salaries are at or above the highest levels in the industry for each role. This approach allows Netflix to attract top performers and eliminates the need for annual raises or bonuses. Instead, employees' compensation is reviewed and adjusted annually based on their market value. This transparent and flexible system ensures that employees are always compensated fairly and competitively.

In addition to high base salaries, Netflix offers a comprehensive benefits package that includes unlimited vacation time, flexible work arrangements, and a generous parental leave policy. The company also provides stock options to all full-time employees, aligning their interests with the long-term success of the organization. Netflix's visionary leadership connects this compensation model to its overall strategy of fostering a high-performance culture and innovation. By offering top-tier compensation and benefits, Netflix communicates to employees that they are valued and empowers them to take risks and contribute to the company's ambitious goals. This approach has helped Netflix attract and retain some of the best talents in the industry, contributing to its continued growth and success in the competitive streaming market.

## Strategy 10: Regularly Review and Improve Hiring Practices

The strategy of continuously evaluating and refining the hiring process is key to improving long-term outcomes. This can be implemented by collecting data on various hiring metrics, including turnover rates, job performance, and employee satisfaction. By analyzing this data, organizations can identify areas for improvement and adjust their hiring strategies to address weaknesses. For adaptive leadership, it's important to remain flexible, ready to implement new approaches as the organization's needs change or as employee feedback highlights areas for refinement.

## Real-World Example: Johnson & Johnson

Johnson & Johnson, the multinational corporation known for its medical devices, pharmaceuticals, and consumer packaged goods, has implemented a comprehensive strategy to regularly review and improve its hiring practices. This approach exemplifies Strategy 10 by leveraging data analytics and adaptive leadership to refine their recruitment processes continuously.

In 2015, Johnson & Johnson launched a data-driven initiative to enhance its hiring practices. The company began by collecting and analyzing various metrics, including time-to-hire, cost-per-hire, quality of hire, and employee retention rates. They also implemented regular surveys to gather feedback from both new hires and hiring managers about their experiences with the recruitment process. This wealth of data allowed J&J to identify areas for improvement and make data-informed decisions about their hiring strategies.

One significant outcome of this initiative was the implementation of AI-powered tools to enhance candidate screening and reduce bias in the hiring process. J&J developed a custom algorithm that analyzes job descriptions for potentially biased language and suggests more inclusive alternatives. The company also introduced video interviewing technology that uses AI to assess candidates' soft skills, complementing traditional evaluation methods. These innovations have led to a more diverse candidate pool and improved hiring outcomes. J&J's adaptive leadership approach ensures that they continue to evolve their hiring practices based on ongoing data analysis and feedback, demonstrating their commitment to continuous improvement in talent acquisition.

## Addressing Challenges: Strategies for Effective Hiring

Implementing new hiring practices can be a daunting task, but it's an investment in your company's future that you can't afford to overlook. You'll likely face resistance to change, resource limitations, and challenges in assessing cultural fit. You might struggle to balance speed with quality in your hiring process, or grapple with unconscious biases that could affect your decisions. In larger organizations, you may find it difficult to maintain consistency across teams, and in today's competitive job market, you'll need to meet increasingly high candidate expectations.

But don't let these challenges deter you. By tackling them head-on, you're setting your company up for long-term success. Start by clearly communicating the benefits of new hiring practices to your team, using data to support your case. Prioritize the most critical changes and implement them gradually as resources allow. Utilize tools and techniques to assess cultural fit and mitigate unconscious bias. Establish clear guidelines and regular audits to ensure consistency, and focus on creating a compelling employer brand that attracts top talent. Remember, overcoming these hurdles isn't just about filling positions—it's about building a strong, capable workforce that will drive your company forward. The effort you put in now will pay dividends in the future, so roll up your sleeves and get started on transforming your hiring practices today.

## Conclusion & Key Takeaways

Strategic hiring is crucial for minimizing turnover and boosting employee retention. When done right, it aligns candidates' skills, values, and expectations with the organization's needs and culture.

Implementing effective hiring can be tough. Common hurdles include resistance to change from HR and management, limited resources for thorough processes, and the challenge of assessing cultural fit while balancing speed and quality. Unconscious bias

can also creep in, alongside the need for consistency across departments and meeting high candidate expectations in a competitive market.

## Key Takeaways

- **The importance of hiring right:** Effective hiring is the cornerstone of employee retention. It sets the stage for everything else, from communication to rewards to development.

- **The consequences of hiring wrong:** Hiring the wrong people can lead to decreased productivity, increased turnover costs, a toxic work environment, and damage to the company's reputation.

- **The benefits of hiring right:** Effective hiring practices can lead to improved employee engagement, satisfaction, loyalty, and a positive reputation.

- **Strategies for hiring right:** The chapter outlines several strategies for hiring right, including defining clear job roles, focusing on cultural fit, implementing structured interviews, leveraging data-driven tools, prioritizing diversity and inclusion, enhancing onboarding, engaging in continuous feedback, building a strong employer brand, offering competitive compensation, and regularly reviewing hiring practices.

- **Addressing challenges:** The chapter also addresses potential challenges in implementing new hiring practices, such as resistance to change, resource limitations, and challenges in assessing cultural fit. It provides strategies for overcoming these hurdles and achieving long-term success.

## Now It's Times to Take Action:

1. **Assess your current hiring process**: Identify any gaps or inefficiencies.

2. **Engage your team**: Involve HR, management, and current employees in refining practices.

3. **Implement changes**: Start with impactful strategies like improving job descriptions or cultural fit assessments.

4. **Monitor and adapt**: Regularly review the outcomes of your hiring process and make adjustments as needed.

## Resources

To deepen your understanding and gain more insights, consider exploring the following resources:

## Books:

1. <u>Who</u> by Geoff Smart and Randy Street: Offers a structured approach to hiring, focusing on identifying and securing top talent.

2. <u>Topgrading, 3rd Edition: The Proven Hiring and Promoting Method that Turbocharges Company Performance</u> by Bradford D. Smart: Provides a

comprehensive system for hiring A-players and improving overall organizational performance.

3. Work Rules!: Insights from Inside Google That Will Transform How You Live and Lead by Laszlo Bock: Explores Google's innovative hiring practices and how they contribute to high employee engagement and low turnover.

4. Hiring for Attitude: A Revolutionary Approach to Recruiting and Selecting People with Both Tremendous Skills and Superb Attitude by Mark Murphy: Focuses on the importance of attitude in hiring, which can be a key predictor of long-term success and retention.

## Articles:

1. How Much is That Bad Hire Really Costing Your Business by Business News Daily: Examines the financial and productivity costs associated with poor hiring decisions and offers solutions to avoid them.

2. Follow These Seven Steps to Ensure You Hire the Right People for Your Team by Forbes: Discusses practical steps for improving hiring practices, including how to assess candidates' fit with company culture.

## Sample Reflection Questions

To help you and your team reflect on your hiring practices and identify areas for improvement, consider these questions:

1.  How well do your current hiring practices align with the strategies outlined in this chapter? Are there any areas where your organization could improve?

2.  How effectively does your organization assess cultural fit during the hiring process? Are there any specific tools or techniques you could implement to enhance this process?

3.  What steps have you taken to promote diversity and inclusion in your hiring practices? Are there any areas where your organization could make improvements?

4.  How effective is your onboarding process? Are new hires adequately prepared for their roles and integrated into the company culture?

5.  How do you provide feedback and support for new hires during their initial months of employment? Are there any opportunities for improvement in this area?

6.  How does your organization's employer brand align with the values and culture you want to convey to potential candidates? Are there any areas where you could strengthen your employer brand?

7.  Are your compensation and benefits packages competitive with other organizations in your industry? How do you ensure that employees feel valued and rewarded for their contributions?

8.  How do you use data to inform your hiring decisions? Are there any opportunities to leverage data more effectively?

9.  Have you encountered resistance to changes in your hiring practices? How have you addressed this resistance?

10. How do you believe the improvements you make to your hiring practices will contribute to the long-term success of your organization?

# CHAPTER 3

# Pillar 2 - Data-Driven Decisions: Using Metrics For Retention Success

———————◆◆◆———————

In today's data-driven world, gut feelings and hunches just don't cut it anymore when it comes to keeping your best talent on board. Think about it: would you rather make decisions about your team's future based on a hunch, or on solid, actionable data?

That's where the power of metrics comes in. By leveraging the right data, you can transform your retention strategies from guesswork into a science.

In this chapter, we're diving deep into the world of data-driven decisions for retention success. We'll explore how to establish and maintain effective employee performance management systems, and we'll uncover methods for monitoring absenteeism that go beyond just counting sick days. By the end of this chapter, you'll have the tools to turn raw data into retention-boosting strategies that will keep your top talent right where they belong - with you.

## Case Study: Walmart's Data-Driven Approach to Employee Retention

Walmart, the retail giant, faced a daunting challenge with employee turnover rates soaring as high as 65% in certain departments. Recognizing the hefty price tag associated with this revolving door of staff, they decided to tackle the problem head-on using a data-driven approach. They rolled out a comprehensive data analysis program, digging into everything from employee surveys and attendance records to performance metrics and career progression data. It was like putting their workforce under a microscope, looking for patterns that the human eye might miss.

What they uncovered was eye-opening. The data revealed that employees who felt underappreciated or couldn't see a clear path for career advancement were the most likely to jump ship. Armed with these insights, Walmart sprang into action. They launched targeted retention strategies for at-risk employees, including personalized recognition programs and clearer communication about internal career opportunities. Managers underwent training to better support their teams, and the company revamped its training programs to focus on skill development and internal mobility.

The results? Nothing short of impressive. Within just one year, overall employee turnover plummeted by 30%. Employee engagement scores shot up, and there was a noticeable uptick in internal promotions. This success story isn't just about Walmart - it's a powerful demonstration of how data analytics can transform employee retention efforts. By basing decisions on hard data rather than assumptions, Walmart not only stemmed the tide of departures but also created a more stable, satisfied workforce. It's a reminder that when it comes to keeping your best people, sometimes the answer lies in the numbers.

## The Science Behind Data Analytics and Predictive Modeling in Employee Retention

We've all heard the saying, "What gets measured gets managed." But in the world of employee retention, it's more like "What gets analyzed gets optimized." Let's dive into the science behind using data to keep your best talent on board.

At its core, data analytics in HR is about turning mountains of information into actionable insights. It's like having a crystal ball that helps you predict which employees might be thinking about leaving before they even know it themselves. Pretty cool, right?

Predictive modeling, a key component of this approach, uses historical data to forecast future behavior. These models can identify patterns and risk factors that human managers might miss, giving you a head start on retention efforts.

The power of this approach lies in its ability to uncover hidden connections. For example, a study by Bersin by Deloitte found that companies using sophisticated data analytics in HR are twice as likely to improve their recruiting efforts and leadership pipelines.

But it's not just about predicting who might leave - it's about understanding why. By analyzing various data points, from performance metrics to engagement survey results, companies can pinpoint the factors that truly drive employee satisfaction and retention.

And the results speak for themselves. According to a study by Nucleus Research, companies that use data analytics in HR see a return on investment of $13.01 for every dollar spent. That's a pretty impressive return on your data investment!

Moreover, the use of data analytics in retention strategies aligns with the psychological concept of "perceived organizational support." When employees see that their company is using data to understand and address their needs, they feel more valued and supported, which in turn increases their commitment to the organization.

So, is it any wonder that data-driven decisions lead to better retention rates? If you're able to predict potential issues, understand the root causes of dissatisfaction, and take proactive steps to keep your employees engaged, why would they want to leave?

The science behind data analytics and predictive modeling shows us that it has the power to transform how we approach employee retention. It turns guesswork into strategy, hunches into actionable insights. To keep improving, companies should invest in robust data collection systems, train HR professionals in data analysis, and create a culture of data-driven decision making.

Remember, in the world of employee retention, knowledge truly is power. And with the right data at your fingertips, you have the power to create a workplace where people don't just stay - they thrive.

## Retention100™: Unveiling Your Data-Driven Retention Strategies

Pillar 2 (items 7-18) of the Retention100™ provides a comprehensive assessment of your organization's use of metrics and data-driven approaches to support employee retention. It encourages you to:

- Calculate and communicate turnover rates at departmental and location levels, providing a clear picture of retention challenges across the organization.

- Monitor attrition and absenteeism based on worker performance and potential, with a focus on high-potential employees who might be at risk of leaving.

- Track absenteeism by department and region, recognizing it as a potential early indicator of turnover.

- Evaluate managers' promotion potential based on their history of developing employees and their team's retention rates.

- Stay informed about the latest research and best practices in staff retention, applying these findings to your organization.

Pillar 2 also explores how your organization uses data to inform decision-making and drive accountability, examining whether:

- Annual evaluations of turnover rates are performed for each department and location, with results shared among senior managers.

- Department-specific turnover charts are displayed within each department, promoting transparency and awareness.

- Protected class worker turnover is monitored and compared to overall organizational turnover, with action taken to address any disparities.

With the Retention100™'s thorough evaluation of your data-driven retention practices, you'll gain a clear understanding of your organization's strengths and weaknesses in using metrics for retention success. This empowers you to pinpoint areas for improvement and implement targeted, data-informed strategies that enhance employee retention and overall organizational performance.

## The Cost of Neglect: When Data Goes Dark

When you don't leverage metrics and analytics for retention, you're essentially flying blind. You might not see the storm clouds gathering until it's too late. Employee dissatisfaction can simmer under the surface, undetected by managers who aren't equipped with the right data.

Ignoring the power of data analytics is like throwing away your GPS in unfamiliar territory. You'll miss early warning signs of turnover, fail to identify patterns in absenteeism, and overlook opportunities to retain high-potential employees. Before you know it, your top talent will be heading for the exit, leaving you scrambling to fill critical roles.

Without data-driven insights, your retention efforts become a costly game of trial and error. You might invest time and resources into initiatives that don't move the needle, while overlooking the real issues driving employee turnover. It's like trying to fix a leak without knowing where the pipe is broken.

The ripple effects of neglecting data in retention strategies extend far beyond your current workforce. In the age of Glassdoor and LinkedIn, word spreads quickly about companies that fail to understand and address employee needs. Your employer brand could take a hit, making it harder to attract new talent and potentially impacting your customer base.

These consequences aren't just about losing a few employees; they can shake your entire organization to its core. The costs of constant recruiting, onboarding, and lost productivity can quickly spiral out of control. Factor in the loss of institutional knowledge and team cohesion, and you're looking at a significant impact on your bottom line.

In the end, the cost of neglecting data-driven retention strategies far outweighs any perceived savings in time or resources. Don't let your organization become a cautionary tale. Embrace the power of data to keep your workforce engaged, productive, and loyal.

## The Benefits of Improvement: Harnessing the Power of Data

As a leader, embracing data-driven retention strategies isn't just following a trend - it's a game-changer that can revolutionize your organization's success. By leveraging analytics, you're not just reacting to problems; you're preventing them before they occur. This proactive approach allows you to tailor your retention initiatives to specific employee segments, boosting engagement and satisfaction. When your team sees that you're using data to understand and address their needs, it fosters a culture of transparency and trust, increasing their loyalty and commitment to your organization.

The benefits of this data-driven approach extend far beyond employee satisfaction. You'll see significant financial gains through reduced turnover costs, increased productivity, and enhanced innovation. Companies excelling in HR analytics have reported 30% higher stock prices and 56% higher profit margins than their competitors. Moreover, your reputation for evidence-based HR practices will make your company a magnet for top talent, giving you a crucial edge in the competitive job market. By harnessing the power of data, you're creating a win-win situation: happier employees, more efficient operations, and a healthier bottom line. So, are you ready to take your retention efforts to the next level? Let's explore how you can use data to transform your organization's future.

## Strategies for Elevating Your Data-Driven Retention Efforts

1. Develop a Comprehensive Data Strategy

2. Implement Advanced Technology Solutions

3. Enhance Processes and Controls

4. Focus on Data Quality and Governance

5. Align with Broader Business Strategy

6. Invest in Talent and Training

7. Prioritize Transparency and Compliance

8. Conduct Regular Assessments

## Strategy 1: Develop a Comprehensive Data Strategy

The first step in crafting your data strategy involves conducting a thorough assessment of your current systems and data sources. This audit will help you pinpoint gaps in your data collection processes and reveal what additional information you need for effective retention analysis. For instance, you may find that while you have solid performance metrics, you're lacking crucial engagement data or insights from exit interviews.

Once you've identified these needs, the next step is integration. Many organizations have valuable employee data scattered across various systems, such as HR information systems and performance management tools. By consolidating this data, you can gain a holistic view of your workforce and uncover insights that might otherwise remain hidden.

Finally, invest in analytics tools that can help interpret this integrated data and generate actionable insights. This way, you'll not only enhance your understanding of employee dynamics but also foster an environment where retention becomes a shared priority across the organization.

## Real-World Example: Stitch Fix

Stitch Fix, the online personal styling service, has masterfully woven data into the very fabric of its business model, creating a tapestry of customer retention that's as intricate as it is effective. At the heart of their strategy is a comprehensive data approach that pulls threads from multiple sources - customer profiles, purchase history, feedback data, stylist notes, and even external fashion trends. This rich tapestry of information allows Stitch Fix to create a holistic view of each customer, tailoring their service with the precision of a master clothier.

But Stitch Fix doesn't just collect data; they put it to work. Their algorithm acts like a skilled stylist, combining all available information to select items that match each customer's unique preferences. This data-driven approach extends beyond just picking the right clothes. It allows Stitch Fix to predict which customers might be at risk of churning, optimize their inventory management, and continuously refine the overall customer experience.

The results of this data-centric strategy speak for themselves. Stitch Fix boasts impressive customer retention rates, with many customers actually increasing their purchase frequency over time. In the cutthroat world of fashion retail, Stitch Fix's ability to leverage data for personalization has become their secret weapon, setting them apart from the competition. It's a powerful reminder that in the world of customer retention, data isn't just numbers - it's the key to unlocking long-lasting customer relationships.

## Strategy 2: Implement Advanced Technology Solutions

By leveraging cutting-edge analytics tools and AI-powered platforms, you can transform your HR department from a reactive cost center into a proactive, strategic powerhouse. These technologies allow you to uncover hidden patterns in your workforce data, predict potential retention risks, and take targeted action before issues escalate, giving you a significant edge in the battle for top talent.

That said, implementing this strategy requires a thoughtful approach. Start by assessing your current tech stack and identifying gaps in your capabilities. Then, clearly define your requirements for a new system, considering factors like data integration capabilities, reporting features, and predictive analytics. As you explore AI-powered solutions, prioritize user-friendliness and scalability to ensure the technology can grow with your organization. Don't forget to evaluate data security features, plan for seamless integration with existing systems, and invest in comprehensive training for your team.

### Real-World Example: Workday

Panasonic, the global electronics giant, faced a common challenge in today's complex business landscape: a patchwork of disparate HR systems spread across its worldwide operations. Recognizing the need for a unified approach, Panasonic made a bold move by implementing Workday's cloud-based human capital management system. This decision wasn't just about streamlining processes; it was a strategic play to revolutionize their approach to employee management and retention.

Workday's platform acted like a powerful magnet, pulling together data from multiple legacy systems to create a single source of truth for employee information. This consolidation unlocked a treasure trove of insights, enabling Panasonic to dive deep into workforce trends and identify retention risks before they became real problems. The platform's self-service features didn't just reduce the administrative burden on HR; they actively improved employee engagement, making staff feel more connected and in control of their work lives. Perhaps most importantly, the real-time reporting and predictive analytics empowered managers to make data-driven decisions about their teams, allowing them to spot and address potential issues before they led to turnover.

By embracing this advanced technology solution, Panasonic didn't just improve its HR operations; it fundamentally changed its approach to talent management. The company reported significant improvements in efficiency, strategic workforce planning, and its ability to retain top talent. Panasonic's success story serves as a blueprint for other organizations looking to move beyond spreadsheets and into the future of HR management and employee retention.

## Strategy 3: Enhance Processes and Controls

Having data and advanced technology is great, but without the right processes and controls in place, it's like trying to drive a sports car on a dirt road - you're not going to get very far. It's time to pave the way for success by taking a hard look at your current processes and implementing tech-enabled solutions that can keep you agile and compliant. This isn't just about ticking boxes for compliance; it's about creating a systematic approach to retention that can be sustained and improved over time.

To put this strategy into action, find the bottlenecks, inefficiencies, and compliance gaps - these are your potholes on the road to retention success. Then, design your ideal retention management process, considering both efficiency and compliance requirements. Leverage technology to automate data collection, analysis, and reporting, freeing up your HR team to focus on more strategic initiatives. Establish clear controls by defining roles, responsibilities, and approval processes for retention-related decisions. Don't forget to implement regular audits and create a feedback loop for continuous improvement. And remember, even the best processes are only as good as the people using them, so make sure to train your team thoroughly.

## Real-World Example: Deloitte

Deloitte, one of the "Big Four" accounting giants, recognized that their talent management processes needed a serious upgrade to keep pace with the rapidly evolving business landscape. They embarked on a full-scale reimagining of their approach to talent management and retention.

As a result of implementing tech-enabled solutions, integrating data from various sources, and introducing a continuous feedback system, Deloitte created a holistic view of each employee's performance, skills, and career aspirations. They replaced the outdated annual performance reviews with a more dynamic, real-time approach. The introduction of predictive analytics allowed them to spot retention risks before they became actual departures.

The payoff? Improved employee engagement, more effective talent development, and better retention of top performers.

## Strategy 4: Focus on Data Quality and Governance

The old adage "garbage in, garbage out" couldn't be more true when it comes to HR analytics. You can have the most sophisticated tools and well-designed processes, but if your underlying data is inaccurate, inconsistent, or insecure, your retention efforts are doomed from the start.

So, how do you ensure your data is rock-solid? Start by establishing clear data standards across all your HR systems. Implement automated validation tools to catch errors at the point of entry. Create a comprehensive data dictionary so everyone's on the same page about what your metrics mean. Assign data stewards to be the guardians of data quality in different areas. Set up robust access controls and security measures to protect sensitive employee information. And don't forget regular data audits

- think of them as health check-ups for your data. Finally, make sure everyone handling HR data understands the importance of quality and governance through thorough training and communication. Focus on these aspects, and you'll create a trustworthy foundation for critical business decisions that can make or break your retention efforts.

## Real-World Example: Philips

Philips, the global health technology giant, recognized that in the world of HR analytics and retention strategies, data isn't just king - it's the entire kingdom. They embarked on a comprehensive data governance initiative. At its core was a robust framework for assessing and improving HR data quality across their global operations. They didn't stop there - Philips created a centralized HR data repository, ensuring consistent data definitions and standards across the organization. They implemented a data stewardship program, assigning data quality responsibilities to specific individuals in each business unit. Automated data validation tools were deployed to catch errors at the point of entry, and stringent data privacy controls were put in place to ensure compliance with global regulations.

As a result, Philips reported significant improvements in the accuracy and reliability of its HR data, leading to more effective workforce planning and retention strategies. Their advanced HR analytics platform could now aggregate and analyze data from diverse sources while maintaining data quality and security. This wasn't just about having better numbers - it was about having better insights. Philips was now able to identify retention risks early and take proactive measures. By investing in training programs to create a culture of data quality awareness among HR staff and managers, they ensured that this wasn't just a one-time fix, but a sustainable change in how they approached HR data.

## Strategy 5: Align with Broader Business Strategy

In the grand chess game of business, your retention strategy shouldn't be a lone pawn - it needs to be a key player working in harmony with your organization's master plan. It's time to elevate your retention efforts from a standalone HR initiative to a strategic driver of business success. This isn't just about keeping employees for the sake of stability; it's about ensuring that the talent you retain and develop is directly contributing to your company's most critical objectives. When your retention strategy aligns with your broader business goals, you're not just playing defense against turnover - you're playing offense, propelling your entire organization forward.

So, how do you make this alignment happen? Start by ensuring your HR team has a deep understanding of the organization's overall strategy and key objectives. Map out how improved retention can contribute to each of these goals. Align your retention metrics with broader business KPIs, and collaborate closely with other departments to understand their talent needs. Regularly communicate the value of your retention efforts to leadership, showing how they're contributing to business goals. Be prepared to adapt your strategies as business objectives evolve. Remember, this isn't a one-time effort - it's an ongoing process of ensuring that your retention strategy remains a key player in your organization's success story so that you're not just keeping employees - you're keeping the right employees.

## Real-World Example: Microsoft

When Satya Nadella took the helm as CEO of Microsoft in 2014, he didn't just see a tech giant in need of a refresh - he saw an opportunity to revolutionize the company's entire approach to talent and innovation. Nadella introduced the concept of a "growth mindset" as a core part of Microsoft's business strategy, emphasizing learning, innovation, and adaptability. This was a fundamental shift in how Microsoft viewed its most valuable asset: its people. The company invested heavily in learning and development programs, revamped its performance management system to focus on individual growth, and emphasized internal mobility to allow employees to gain new experiences.

Microsoft saw significant improvements in employee engagement and retention, particularly among high-performers. But the impact went far beyond just keeping people around. This alignment of talent strategy with business strategy contributed to Microsoft's impressive business turnaround, with the company's market value tripling in the five years following the introduction of the growth mindset approach. By tying retention metrics to broader business metrics, Microsoft demonstrated how improved retention and employee growth directly contributed to innovation and market success.

## Strategy 6: Invest in Talent and Training

Your most valuable asset isn't your cutting-edge technology or your mountain of data - it's your people. As we shift towards more data-driven and tech-enabled retention strategies, it's crucial to invest in upskilling your team to handle these new challenges. This isn't just about teaching new skills; it's about fostering a culture of continuous learning and adaptation. By empowering your HR team with the knowledge and skills they need to leverage new technologies and data analysis techniques, you're not just improving your retention strategies - you're future-proofing your entire HR function.

So, how do you put this strategy into action? Start by conducting a thorough assessment of your team's current skills and identify areas for improvement. Develop comprehensive training programs that cover both technical skills like data analysis and HR tech, and soft skills like change management and strategic thinking. Encourage cross-functional learning by fostering collaboration between HR, IT, and finance teams. Provide hands-on experience through real retention projects, and support continuous learning through workshops, conferences, and online courses. Create a knowledge-sharing culture where team members can exchange learnings and best practices. And don't forget to measure the impact of these initiatives regularly.

Remember, investing in your people isn't just about improving your retention strategies - it's about building a more capable, adaptable, and innovative HR function that can drive your organization's success well into the future.

### Real-World Example: AT&T

AT&T's Workforce 2020 initiative, launched in 2013, stands as a shining example of how investing in talent and training can revolutionize a company's approach to retention and business transformation. Recognizing the rapid evolution of the telecommunications industry, AT&T embarked on a massive reskilling program designed to prepare its 280,000 employees for the company's shift from a legacy telephone business to a competitive technology company. This wasn't just about teaching new skills; it was about future-proofing their entire workforce.

The initiative was comprehensive and forward-thinking. AT&T invested $1 billion in a state-of-the-art online learning platform, AT&T University, offering courses ranging from basic technical skills to advanced data science. They partnered with Udacity to create "nanodegrees" in high-demand fields and developed career intelligence tools to help employees understand which skills were in demand.

The results were impressive: by 2020, AT&T had reduced its product-development cycle time by 40%, accelerated time to revenue by 32%, and filled 40% of its technology management jobs with internal candidates. This initiative demonstrates how a strategic investment in talent and training can drive significant business value while simultaneously improving employee retention and engagement. By fostering a culture of continuous learning and adaptability, AT&T not only prepared for the future but also created a more loyal and capable workforce.

## Strategy 7: Prioritize Transparency and Compliance

When employees feel they're in the loop about company practices and understand how their roles contribute to the bigger picture, they're more likely to stick around. This openness cultivates an environment where employees feel valued and respected, which can significantly boost loyalty. Coupled with a strong commitment to compliance, this strategy ensures that your organization isn't just meeting legal requirements, but also aligning with ethical standards that resonate with your workforce.

So, how do you put this into practice? Start by developing clear channels for sharing information about company policies, performance metrics, and retention initiatives. Be transparent about how employee data is collected and used in retention efforts. Ensure your HR staff and managers are well-versed in relevant labor laws and conduct regular audits of your retention practices. Implement processes that prioritize ethical considerations in retention-related decisions and create safe channels for employees to provide feedback or report concerns. Regularly share retention metrics and initiatives with your team, demonstrating your commitment to improvement. Remember, prioritizing transparency and compliance isn't just about following rules - it's about creating a culture of trust and respect that makes employees want to stay for the long haul.

## Real-World Example: Heineken

Heineken, the global brewing giant, has tapped into the power of transparency and compliance to create a workplace culture that's as refreshing as their beer. They've established a robust system of open communication channels, including regular town hall meetings where leadership shares company updates and future strategies. This openness extends to their policies on diversity, inclusion, and environmental sustainability, ensuring employees have a clear understanding of the company's values and commitments. Heineken doesn't just talk the talk - they walk the walk by providing comprehensive compliance training programs and actively soliciting employee feedback through surveys and focus groups.

The results of Heineken's transparency efforts are as satisfying as a cold brew on a hot day. The company enjoys high employee satisfaction rates and low turnover levels compared to industry averages. Employees feel a strong sense of belonging within the organization, driven by the company's transparent culture and commitment to ethical practices. By regularly sharing progress on key performance indicators related to employee engagement and retention, Heineken reinforces its commitment to continuous improvement.

## Strategy 8: Conduct Regular Assessment

In the world of employee retention, staying static is a recipe for falling behind. That's why conducting regular assessments of your retention strategies, data practices, and technologies is crucial.

These ongoing evaluations ensure that your approach remains effective, compliant, and in sync with both your organizational goals and the ever-changing needs of your workforce. It's not just about identifying what's not working; it's about continuously refining and improving your retention efforts to stay ahead of the curve.

To implement this strategy effectively, start by setting up a consistent schedule for these assessments. Gather diverse feedback from various stakeholders, including HR, management, and employees themselves. Regularly review your retention metrics and compare them against industry benchmarks. Stay informed about changes in labor laws, industry trends, and best practices in retention. Don't be afraid to test new approaches on a small scale, and be prepared to adapt quickly based on your findings.

## Real-World Example: Novo Nordisk

Novo Nordisk, the global healthcare giant specializing in diabetes care, has turned regular assessments into an art form when it comes to driving continuous improvement in retention strategies. Their approach is comprehensive and dynamic, involving annual retention audits, frequent "pulse" surveys for real-time feedback, regular evaluations of HR technologies, and consistent benchmarking against industry standards. They've even mastered the delicate balance of maintaining global standards while allowing for local adaptations based on regional assessments.

Not surprisingly, the company consistently reports employee turnover rates that are well below industry averages, and they've seen year-over-year improvements in employee engagement scores. Interestingly, employees often cite the company's commitment to continuous improvement as a key factor in their job satisfaction.

Novo Nordisk's approach shows that the key to success lies not just in conducting assessments, but in actively using those insights to drive meaningful improvements.

## Addressing Challenges: Navigating the Data-Driven Retention Landscape

As you embark on your journey to implement data-driven retention strategies, it's essential to recognize that while these approaches hold great promise, they also come with challenges. Understanding and addressing these hurdles will allow you to create a more effective and robust retention strategy.

Start by overcoming data-related barriers such as ensuring data quality, addressing privacy concerns, and managing resistance to change. Implement rigorous data validation processes and regular audits to maintain high-quality data, as poor data can lead to flawed insights. Additionally, be transparent about how you handle employee data, especially in light of increasing privacy regulations. This transparency fosters trust and ensures that employees feel secure about their personal information.

Another significant challenge is managing the overwhelming amount of data available today. To navigate this information deluge, focus on identifying key retention metrics that are most relevant to your organization. Instead of trying to analyze everything at once, concentrate on a handful of metrics that can provide the majority of insights. Investing in advanced analytics tools can also help you make sense of large datasets and identify patterns that may not be immediately obvious. Furthermore, developing data literacy across your organization is crucial; consider training programs that empower your team to interpret and utilize data effectively. Remember, while data is a powerful ally in your retention strategy, it should complement human insight rather than replace it.

## Conclusion & Key Takeaways

Data-driven decisions are the new frontier of retention. By harnessing the power of metrics and analytics, you're not just playing defense against turnover; you're playing offense, propelling your organization forward. But remember, data is just a tool. It's the insights you glean from it that truly matter. The key is to ask the right questions, to look beyond the obvious, and to use data as a springboard for innovation. Don't be afraid to experiment, to fail, and to learn. The journey of data-driven retention is a continuous one, filled with opportunities for growth and discovery.

## Key Takeaways

1. **Data is your superpower:** Use it to understand your workforce, predict retention risks, and make informed decisions.

2. **Don't just collect data; analyze it:** Look for patterns, trends, and insights that can inform your retention strategies.

3. **Focus on key metrics:** Don't get overwhelmed by data overload. Identify the metrics that matter most and focus on them.

4. **Align your retention strategy with your broader business goals:** Ensure that your efforts are contributing to your organization's overall success.

5. **Invest in talent and technology:** Empower your HR team with the skills and tools they need to succeed.

6. **Prioritize transparency and compliance:** Build a culture of trust and respect that fosters employee loyalty.

7. **Conduct regular assessments:** Continuously evaluate and refine your retention strategies.

### Now it's time to take action!

Begin by assessing your current data capabilities and retention practices. Identify areas where you can start implementing or improving data-driven strategies. Choose one or two key initiatives from this chapter and develop a concrete plan for implementation.

Remember to involve key stakeholders from across the organization in this process.

Engage in ongoing dialogue with your IT, HR, and business intelligence teams to ensure you're leveraging the full potential of your data. Regularly review and refine your approach based on the results and feedback you receive.

When you harness the power of data to inform your retention strategies, you're not just keeping employees—you're creating a more engaged, productive, and loyal workforce that can drive your organization's success for years to come. The journey to data-driven retention may be challenging, but the rewards are well worth the effort.

## Resources

For those interested in further exploring the topic of data-driven retention strategies, we recommend the following resources:

## Books:

1. <u>People Analytics in the Era of Big Data: Changing the Way You Attract, Acquire, Develop, and Retain Talent</u> by Jean Paul Isson and Jesse S. Harriott: A comprehensive guide to leveraging data for HR decision-making.

2. <u>The Power of People: Learn How Successful Organizations Use Workforce Analytics To Improve Business Performance</u> by Nigel Guenole, Jonathan Ferrar, and Sheri Feinzig: Insights into implementing workforce analytics successfully.

3. <u>Predictive HR Analytics: Mastering the HR Metric</u> by Dr. Martin Edwards and Kirsten Edwards: A practical guide to using analytics in HR processes.

## Online Tools:

1. <u>Visier</u>: An end-to-end people analytics and workforce planning solution.

2. <u>Tableau</u>: A powerful data visualization tool that can be used for HR analytics.

3. <u>IBM Watson Analytics for HR</u>: An AI-powered analytics platform designed specifically for HR.

4. <u>Workday People Analytics</u>: An analytics solution integrated with Workday's HRIS.

## Sample Reflection Questions

1. How can the use of metrics and data analytics enhance your organization's retention efforts?

2. What specific data points would you find most valuable in understanding and addressing employee retention challenges?

3. How can you ensure that your organization's data is accurate, reliable, and accessible for analysis?

4. What are some key metrics that can be used to assess employee retention and engagement?

5. How can you use data to identify potential retention risks and take proactive measures?

6. What are the potential benefits of using predictive modeling in HR?

7. How can you apply the lessons learned from Walmart's data-driven approach to retention in your own organization?

8. What are some strategies for enhancing data-driven decision making within your HR team?

9. How can you ensure that your retention strategies are aligned with your broader business objectives?

10. What are the potential challenges in implementing data-driven retention strategies, and how can you overcome them?

# CHAPTER 4

# Pillar 3 - The Power of Communication: Keeping Employees Engaged

―――――⁂―――――

Communication about building relationships, fostering trust, and creating a sense of belonging. Think about it: when you feel heard, valued, and informed, you're more likely to stick around, right?

In this chapter, we're going to explore how communication can be a powerful tool for retaining your employees. We'll talk about creating a culture where everyone's voice is heard, and how to use communication to boost employee satisfaction and loyalty.

## Case Study: Uber's Bumpy Ride

Uber, the multinational ride-sharing company, experienced a tumultuous period marked by communication failures that led to a toxic work culture, public relations crises, and legal battles. The company's environment was characterized by a lack of transparency, siloed information, and retaliation against those who reported misconduct. This toxic atmosphere, coupled with aggressive and unethical business practices, resulted in high turnover rates, damaged reputation, and numerous legal challenges. Uber's leadership failed to address systemic problems related to sexual harassment, corporate governance, and unethical business practices, further exacerbating the issues.

Recognizing the need for change, Uber took significant steps to turn things around. They brought in a new CEO to prioritize transparency, collaboration, and ethical behavior, setting a new tone for the company. Uber also invested in diversity and inclusion initiatives, including employee resource groups, unconscious bias training, and improved hiring processes. To boost communication, they introduced town hall meetings, anonymous feedback platforms, and regular employee engagement surveys. These efforts aimed to create a more inclusive environment where employees felt valued and heard, leading to greater transparency and accountability.

While Uber's journey to recovery is ongoing, the company has already seen improvements in employee satisfaction and lower turnover rates. Uber's experience demonstrates that even companies facing significant challenges can take meaningful steps towards creating a more positive and communicative work environment, ultimately benefiting both employees and the organization as a whole.

## The Science Behind Communication: Building Stronger Teams

The power of effective communication extends beyond individual interactions to shape the overall team dynamic. According to the global management consulting firm McKinsey & Company, well-connected teams can increase their productivity by an impressive 20-25%. This boost in efficiency comes from clearer role definitions, smoother collaboration, and more streamlined problem-solving processes. Furthermore, research shows that effective communication enhances both the speed and accuracy of decision-making, leading to more efficient and precise work outcomes.

A study by SHRM found that companies with effective communication practices experience lower turnover rates. This correlation is unsurprising when considering the multifaceted benefits of good communication: increased connection, engagement, happiness, safety, collaboration, productivity, and improved results.

## The Retention100™: Spilling the Beans on Your Communication Skills

Pillar 3 (items 19–32) of the Retention100™ provides a comprehensive assessment of your organization's communication practices, focusing on its impact on employee retention. It encourages that you:

- Have transparent discussions about metrics like turnover and absenteeism rates in an effort to brainstorm solutions and address them

- Collect employee input through surveys, focus groups, and performance appraisals to gauge how effectively you've addressed staff concerns

- Foster an environment of open communication and transparency through town hall meetings, manager-employee interactions, and cross-functional collaborations.

Pillar 3 also explores how your organization shares its retention efforts with the outside world, examining whether:

- Retention goals and achievements are shared with stakeholders
- External input is sought on retention strategies

With the Retention100™'s thorough evaluation of your communication practices, you'll gain a clear understanding of your organization's strengths and weaknesses, empowering you to pinpoint areas for improvement and implement targeted strategies that bolster employee retention.

## The Cost of Neglect: When Silence Speaks Louder Than Words

You might think that keeping employees in the dark is strategic in some respects. Or maybe communication is restricted to Slack messages and yearly performance reviews. But that's too little, too late.

When you don't communicate often or effectively enough, employee morale takes a nosedive. Uncertainty breeds doubt, and doubt is the enemy of engagement. Don't keep employees guessing; it only breeds speculation.

Poor communication is a one-way ticket to turnover town. Misunderstandings, conflicts, and feeling undervalued are the ultimate deal-breakers. Employees will pack their bags faster than you can say "water cooler talk."

Word travels fast, especially when it's about a bad boss or a company that doesn't listen. Negative vibes spread like wildfire on social media, scaring away potential employees and customers. Your company's reputation is on the line. Don't blow it.

These consequences aren't just about morale; they hit your bottom line hard. Lost productivity and damage control efforts can quickly drain your resources. In the end, the cost of neglecting effective communication is far greater than any perceived benefits of silence.

## The Benefits of Improvement: Reaping the Rewards

We've already mentioned that the right communication can make employees feel heard, valued, and in the know. That's what it takes to turn them from clock watchers to invested stakeholders.

Clear communication is also the grease that keeps the organizational machine running smoothly. It reduces errors, speeds up processes, and turns good ideas into reality.

Finally, a reputation for open and honest communication can help make your company the envy of competitors.

Strong communication, in other words, is a win-win for everyone involved. So if you're serious about making headway, read on as we share three precise strategies you can use.

## Strategies for Turning Insights into Action

1. Embrace Transparency

2. Fueling Engagement Through Feedback

3. Uncovering the Secrets to Staying Power

## Strategy 1: Embrace Transparency

As you navigate the complexities of employee turnover, it's essential to recognize that transparency can be a game-changer for your organization. While turnover is an inevitable part of business, how you manage it can significantly influence your retention rates. Rather than hiding turnover data to maintain morale, consider the benefits of being open about this issue. Research shows that employees desire greater transparency and collaboration in their workplaces. In fact, the Slack Future of Work Study (2018) found that transparent communication leads to job satisfaction levels that are 12 times higher, which in turn fosters increased productivity and lower turnover rates.

To effectively embrace transparency, start by using turnover metrics as your guiding star. Monitor key metrics such as overall turnover rates and departmental statistics to identify trends and problem areas. Delve deeper into understanding the reasons behind employee departures through exit interviews, satisfaction surveys, and pulse surveys.

This data will help you pinpoint specific factors contributing to turnover, such as management styles or workplace culture, allowing you to proactively address these root causes.

Once you've gathered this information, prioritize solutions based on your findings. Implement targeted strategies to improve areas like compensation, training programs, or workplace environment. By keeping your team informed about these changes and involving them in the process, you create a culture of trust and engagement. Embracing transparency not only helps you tackle turnover more effectively but also cultivates a positive work environment where employees feel valued and connected to the organization's goals.

## Real-World Example: Buffer

Buffer, a leading social media management platform, faced the same challenges as many tech companies: high turnover rates. To tackle this issue, Buffer took a bold approach: complete transparency. The company publicly shared its finances, salaries, and even performance reviews, fostering trust and accountability. This open communication created a culture where employees felt empowered and informed, leading to increased job satisfaction and reduced turnover.

By breaking down silos and encouraging open dialogue, Buffer built a work environment where employees felt valued and trusted. This transparency not only improved employee retention but also attracted top talent seeking a more authentic and open company culture. Buffer's success demonstrates the power of transparency in creating a positive and sustainable workplace.

## Strategy 2: Fueling Engagement Through Feedback

As a leader, you hold the key to unlocking your team's full potential through the power of feedback. Think about it - how can your employees excel if they're unsure about their performance or impact? Consistent, constructive feedback is the missing piece that bridges the gap between effort and excellence. Without it, your team members may struggle to understand their value, identify areas for growth, and feel truly connected to your organization's mission. This disconnect can lead to a dangerous spiral of disengagement, decreased productivity, and ultimately, higher turnover rates. It's time to break this cycle and create a culture of open communication and continuous improvement.

To fuel engagement through feedback, start by implementing regular pulse checks and focus groups to gauge employee satisfaction and identify emerging issues. Transform your performance reviews from dreaded critiques into valuable growth opportunities by making them a two-way street for feedback and development. Don't underestimate the power of peer-to-peer recognition - encourage your team to share positive feedback with one another daily. This not only cultivates a culture of appreciation but also provides ongoing input on individual performance. Remember, feedback isn't just about addressing problems; it's about fostering trust, empowering growth, and creating a workplace where every team member feels valued and heard.

## Real-World Example: Adobe

Adobe replaced traditional performance reviews with a "Check-In" process – ongoing feedback and development conversations. These "Check-Ins" focus on goal-setting, growth opportunities, and regular feedback exchanges between employees and managers. As a result, Adobe experienced a 30% reduction in voluntary turnover, increased employee engagement, and improved overall performance.

Fostering a culture of open and honest feedback goes beyond information gathering; it establishes trust and empowers your employees by giving them a voice in shaping their work environment. This approach not only improves communication but also enhances overall job satisfaction, engagement, and retention.

## Strategy 3: Uncovering the Secrets to Staying Power

To boost retention in your organization, one of the most effective strategies is to tap into the insights of your long-term employees. These individuals have navigated various challenges and changes within the company, and their reasons for staying can reveal what truly matters in your workplace culture. By understanding their motivations, you can highlight the elements that foster loyalty and commitment among your workforce.

Start by conducting deep-dive interviews with these seasoned employees. Ask open-ended questions about their experiences and what keeps them motivated. Look for common themes in their responses to identify the key factors contributing to their loyalty. Use these insights to align your company culture and values with what resonates most with your top performers. Remember, long-service employees not only serve as role models but also help preserve institutional knowledge and promote continuity.

### Real-World Example: Marriott International

Marriott International offers a prime example of the power of listening to your long-term employees. Their "Journeys" project, launched in 2013, involved in-depth interviews with seasoned associates to understand the factors driving their loyalty. By sharing these stories, Marriott not only strengthened employee morale but also refined their retention strategies to align with what truly matters to their workforce. When people love where they work, it shows in everything they do – from customer service to innovation.

## Addressing Challenges: Leveling Up Your Communication Game

As a leader, you're undoubtedly aware that effective communication is the cornerstone of any thriving organization. However, you're likely to face numerous hurdles along the way - language barriers, cultural differences, and generational gaps can all throw a wrench in your communication efforts. But don't let these challenges discourage you. Instead, view them as opportunities to elevate your communication game and create a more inclusive, productive work environment.

Start by embracing multilingualism in your workplace. If you have team members who aren't native English speakers or you're working with outsourced talent, consider offering language training. Utilize visuals to enhance understanding and ensure everyone's on the same page. Research consistently shows that companies with diverse executive teams significantly outperform their peers financially. So, celebrate the diversity in your team and leverage it to foster innovation and improve decision-making.

Don't overlook the generational differences in your workforce. Each generation has its own communication preferences - while Baby Boomers might prefer face-to-face meetings, your Gen Z employees might be more comfortable with digital channels. By understanding and accommodating these differences, you can create a communication strategy that resonates with everyone on your team, regardless of their age or background.

When it comes to difficult conversations, preparation is key. Set the stage by choosing a private, comfortable setting and scheduling enough time for an unhurried discussion.

Begin by establishing a shared purpose and finding common ground. Practice active listening, show empathy, and ask open-ended questions to understand the other person's perspective. Express your thoughts assertively without blaming or attacking, using "I" statements to describe your emotions and experiences. Focus on problem-solving by brainstorming potential solutions together. Finally, follow up by summarizing the discussion, clarifying next steps, and expressing gratitude for the other person's willingness to engage.

## Conclusion & Key Takeaways

We've covered a lot of ground, from the science to the strategies. The bottom line is this: communication is the heartbeat of a thriving organization. It's the glue that binds teams, the fuel that ignites innovation, and the key to unlocking employee potential.

## Key Takeaways

Some of the key actions retention-proof companies take include:

1. Recognizing the importance of open, transparent, and empathetic communication in building trust and fostering employee engagement.

2. Implementing regular feedback mechanisms, creating a safe environment for feedback sharing, and acting on employee feedback to address sensitive topics and manage conflicts effectively.

3. Promoting a culture of trust and empowerment by encouraging open and honest dialogue, promoting

psychological safety, and empowering employees to share their perspectives.

4. Cultivating a sense of purpose by clearly communicating the company's mission, vision, and values, aligning individual goals with organizational objectives, and celebrating successes and milestones.

## Now it's time to take action!

We recommend adapting these strategies to your organization's unique needs and culture, with the goal of improving communication and cultivating a supportive work environment. A thriving, engaged, and motivated workforce is a direct result of these efforts.

To ensure your organization consistently maintains a culture of open communication, regularly assess your current practices. Employee surveys, for example, can provide valuable insights into the effectiveness of communication channels, management styles, and overall satisfaction.

Actively seeking and incorporating employee input allows you to refine your communication strategies, ensuring your team feels valued, supported, and connected—essential ingredients for long-term success.

## Resources

To further explore the topics of communication and employee engagement, consider the following books, articles, and online resources:

## Books:

1. Crucial Conversations: Tools for Talking When Stakes Are High by Joseph Grenny, Kerry Patterson, Ron McMillan, Al Switzler, and Emily Gregory:

2. The Lost Art of Listening by Michael P. Nichols: Practical techniques for becoming a more effective listener, which can significantly improve communication and retention.

3. Radical Candor: Be a Kick-Ass Boss Without Losing Your Humanity by Kim Scott: A framework for effective leadership that combines kindness and toughness.

4. Difficult Conversations: How to Discuss What Matters Most by Douglas Stone, Bruce Patton, and Sheila Heen: Practical strategies for handling difficult conversations, which can be essential for addressing conflicts and misunderstandings that can impact employee retention.

## Sample Reflection Questions

1. How can effective communication contribute to a positive and productive work environment?

2. Why is it crucial for organizations to create a culture where everyone's voice is heard?

3. What are the potential consequences of poor communication within an organization?

4. How did communication failures contribute to the negative outcomes faced by Uber?

5. What specific steps could Uber have taken to improve its communication practices and prevent the crises that occurred?

6. How does effective communication impact team dynamics and productivity?

7. What role does communication play in decision-making and problem-solving processes?

8. How can organizations measure the effectiveness of their communication strategies?

9. What specific strategies can organizations implement to improve their communication practices and foster employee engagement?

10. How can leaders create a culture of open and honest communication within their teams?

# CHAPTER 5

# Pillar 4: Recognizing Achievements: Appreciation Fuels Retention

———— ✦ ————

Recognition is more than just a pat on the back. It's the fuel that ignites employee engagement and drives retention. When employees feel valued and appreciated for their contributions, they are more likely to be committed, motivated, and satisfied with their jobs.

This chapter delves into the importance of recognition in creating a positive and supportive work environment. We will explore how effective recognition programs can boost employee morale, enhance job satisfaction, and ultimately improve retention rates. We'll also discuss strategies for implementing recognition programs that resonate with your employees and align with your organization's values.

As a result, you'll see how to develop targeted strategies to foster a culture of appreciation and celebrate your employees' achievements.

## Case Study: PepsiCo

PepsiCo introduced a comprehensive employee recognition program called "PepsiCo Rewards." This platform allows employees to acknowledge and appreciate their peers' contributions and successes by sending thank-you notes, points, and awards.

PepsiCo's program focuses on celebrating diverse achievements, including innovation, customer service, teamwork, and community involvement.

After implementing this recognition program, PepsiCo reported higher employee satisfaction, engagement, and retention rates. The company found that employees who received recognition were more likely to stay with the company and deliver strong performance.

## The Science Behind Recognition: A Retention Catalyst

Recognition isn't just about making employees feel good - it's a powerful psychological tool that directly impacts retention and performance. When employees are acknowledged for their efforts, it triggers a positive reinforcement cycle, encouraging them to repeat desirable behaviors and boosting overall performance and morale. This recognition also fulfills a fundamental human need for belonging and social connection, contributing to a positive self-image, increased motivation, and higher job satisfaction. Maslow's Hierarchy of Needs underscores the importance of esteem needs, including respect and recognition, for psychological well-being. By meeting these needs in the workplace, you're helping your employees feel fulfilled, engaged, and committed to their roles.

Moreover, recognition plays a crucial role in influencing the Employee Net Promoter Score (eNPS), a key measure of employee satisfaction and loyalty. A high eNPS is indicative of a workforce that's not only satisfied but also likely to stay with the company and recommend it to others.

In essence, recognition serves as a powerful retention catalyst, reinforcing positive behaviors, fostering a sense of belonging, fulfilling psychological needs, and ultimately driving employee satisfaction and loyalty.

## The Retention100™: Recognizing Employee Contributions

Pillar 4 (items 34-38) of the Retention100™ assessment focuses on your organization's recognition practices and their impact on employee retention. It encourages you to:

- Acknowledge and celebrate employees who have been with the organization for significant periods.

- Recognize managers who have successfully retained their teams, demonstrating effective leadership and management practices.

- Recognize employees' personal events, such as birthdays and anniversaries, to show appreciation and foster a positive work environment.

- Encourage employees to submit ideas specifically aimed at improving retention, offering incentives for innovative solutions.

- Find meaningful ways to showcase how each employee's work contributes to the organization's mission, fostering a sense of purpose and connection.

These recognition practices of the Retention100™ will help you gain insights into your organization's strengths and weaknesses, enabling you to identify areas for improvement and implement targeted strategies to enhance employee retention.

## The Cost of Neglect: Consequences of Ignoring

Neglecting employee recognition can have detrimental consequences for both employees and the organization as a whole.

When employees feel unappreciated and undervalued, their morale suffers. This can lead to decreased motivation, satisfaction, and increased stress levels, contributing to burnout and mental health issues. Additionally, a lack of recognition can hinder career growth, as employees may not see a clear connection between their performance and advancement opportunities.

Organizations that neglect employee recognition often experience decreased productivity due to disengaged employees. High turnover rates are another consequence, as employees seek companies that value and appreciate their contributions. This leads to increased costs associated with recruiting, hiring, and training new employees.

A study by the Society for Human Resource Management found that 79% of employees who quit their jobs cite a lack of appreciation as a key reason for leaving.

Neglecting employee recognition is a costly oversight, both financially and in terms of employee satisfaction. Recognizing employees' contributions, therefore, is essential for maintaining high morale, productivity, and retention in the workplace.

## The Benefits of Improvement: Reaping the Rewards of Employee Recognition

Recognizing your team's hard work is not just a nice gesture; it's a smart business strategy. When employees feel appreciated, they become more motivated and satisfied, which significantly boosts retention. In fact, research by the Cicero Group shows that companies with strong recognition programs experience a 31% lower turnover rate.

Moreover, nearly 70% of employees indicated they would work harder if their efforts were better acknowledged. By investing in employee recognition, you create a positive work environment that encourages continuous improvement and fosters job satisfaction.

The benefits of recognition extend beyond individual employees; they enhance overall organizational performance. Engaged employees are more productive, which directly contributes to your bottom line. Effective recognition programs also reduce turnover rates, saving your organization recruitment and training costs. Additionally, a culture of appreciation promotes collaboration and innovation, creating a sense of community among team members. Ultimately, recognizing and valuing employee contributions is essential for cultivating high engagement and loyalty.

## Strategies for Improvement: Putting it into Action

1. Service Recognition
2. Personal Events Recognition
3. Empowering Employees Through Suggestion Systems
4. Showcasing Individual Impact

## Strategy 1: Service Recognition

Just as recognizing the value of employee turnover can lead to improved retention strategies, acknowledging and celebrating long-term service can foster a positive and supportive work environment.

Implement a tiered recognition program to reward employees for different tenure milestones, such as 5, 10, and 15 years of service. This demonstrates appreciation for their continued commitment and contributions. Publicly acknowledge long-serving employees at company-wide events, in newsletters, or on social media to inspire others and foster a sense of pride.

Additionally, consider offering personalized gifts or experiences to make rewards more meaningful. Tailor them to individual interests and preferences to show that you value each employee's unique contributions.

Recognize and celebrate your employees' long-term contributions to show your appreciation and create a workplace where people feel valued and loyal.

## Real-World Example: Google

Google has a long-standing tradition of recognizing employee contributions through its "Googler of the Year" award. This prestigious honor is given annually to an employee who has made an exceptional contribution to the company. The award is accompanied by a cash bonus, a trophy, and public recognition.

The "Googler of the Year" award not only celebrates individual achievements but also reinforces Google's culture of innovation, collaboration, and employee empowerment. By recognizing and rewarding top performers, Google fosters a sense of pride, loyalty, and motivation among its employees.

## Strategy 2: Personal Events Recognition

Acknowledging and celebrating employees' personal events can go a long way in fostering a positive and supportive work environment.

Here's how: Set aside some funds to recognize birthdays, anniversaries, and other special occasions. Give employees the freedom to choose how they want to be celebrated, whether it's a gift card, extra time off, or a public shout-out. Encourage your team to recognize and appreciate each other's personal milestones. This creates a stronger sense of community and belonging.

Recognizing personal events shows employees that you care about them as individuals, not just as workers. This can boost morale, loyalty, and overall job satisfaction.

## Real-World Example: Zappos

Zappos, the online retailer known for its exceptional customer service, has a unique program called "Zappys" to recognize employee personal milestones. Employees can submit "Zappy" nominations for their colleagues, and the recipient receives a personalized gift, a public acknowledgement, and a donation to a charity of their choice.

The Zappys program fosters a positive and supportive work culture at Zappos by encouraging employees to recognize and appreciate each other's contributions. It also demonstrates the company's commitment to employee well-being and creates a sense of community within the organization.

Strategy 3: Empowering Employees Through Suggestion Systems

Fostering a culture of continuous improvement and employee empowerment is essential for reducing turnover. Implementing a suggestion system can provide a platform for employees to contribute their ideas and insights.

Make it easy for employees to submit their ideas through a dedicated online platform, suggestion boxes, or regular meetings. Encourage participation by emphasizing the value of their input and the potential impact of their suggestions. Acknowledge all submissions, provide feedback, and reward innovative solutions that lead to positive outcomes. Consider incorporating employee-generated ideas into company policies, initiatives, or projects.

Create a culture where employees feel empowered to share their ideas and are recognized for their contributions. This can foster a positive work environment and improve employee retention and satisfaction.

### Real-World Example: IDEO

IDEO, a leading design and innovation firm, has a well-known employee suggestion program called the "Brainstorming Dojo." This program encourages employees at all levels to share their ideas for improving products, processes, or company culture.

IDEO provides a dedicated platform for employees to submit their ideas anonymously. A team of innovation leaders reviews submissions and provides feedback to the contributors. Ideas that are deemed promising are further developed and potentially implemented.

The Brainstorming Dojo has been instrumental in driving innovation and fostering a culture of continuous improvement at IDEO. Employees feel empowered to share their ideas and see their contributions recognized and valued. This has led to a more engaged, innovative, and supportive workplace culture.

## Strategy 4: Showcasing Individual Impact

As a leader, one of your most powerful tools for fostering employee engagement and loyalty is highlighting the impact of each individual's work. It's not enough to simply assign tasks and expect your team to understand their importance. You need to actively demonstrate how their efforts contribute to the bigger picture. Start by providing personalized annual reports that showcase how each employee's contributions align with your organization's mission and goals.

But don't stop at reports. Use these insights as a springboard for meaningful one-on-one discussions with your employees. These conversations are your opportunity to dive deeper into their achievements, discuss areas for growth, and align on career goals. This is how you create a sense of purpose and belonging that can dramatically improve job satisfaction and retention.

## Real-World Example: Salesforce

Salesforce, the customer relationship management (CRM) software company, hosts an annual event called "Dreamforce" that brings together employees, customers, partners, and industry leaders. At Dreamforce, employees have the opportunity to learn about the company's strategy, connect with colleagues, and celebrate their achievements.

One of the key elements of Dreamforce is the recognition of top-performing employees. Salesforce awards individuals and teams for their outstanding contributions to the company's success. This recognition not only celebrates achievements but also reinforces the company's values and inspires others to strive for excellence.

Dreamforce fosters a culture of collaboration, innovation, and employee empowerment at Salesforce. This event helps employees feel connected to the company's mission, recognize the value of their contributions, and build relationships with their colleagues.

## Overcoming Challenges in Implementing a Recognition Program

As you embark on implementing a robust recognition program, you're likely to encounter some obstacles along the way. But don't let these challenges deter you - with thoughtful planning and proactive measures, you can overcome them and create a powerful tool for boosting employee engagement and retention. One of the most common hurdles you'll face is ensuring consistency in recognition practices. To tackle this, start by establishing clear guidelines and criteria for recognition. Set expectations for the types of behaviors or achievements that should be acknowledged and outline appropriate ways to recognize them. This framework will help create a fair and transparent system that resonates across your organization.

You might also find yourself grappling with budgetary constraints or time limitations. Don't let these factors hold you back. Remember, effective recognition doesn't always require a hefty budget. Prioritize cost-effective methods that still make a meaningful impact, such as personalized, heartfelt gestures like handwritten notes or public acknowledgment. These can be just as powerful as monetary rewards. To address time constraints, look for ways to streamline your recognition process. Integrate it into existing workflows and leverage technology, such as automated reminders or digital platforms, to facilitate timely and efficient acknowledgment of your employees' contributions.

Lastly, be mindful that not all employees are comfortable with public recognition. It's crucial to tailor your efforts to individual preferences and comfort levels. Some team members may thrive on public praise, while others prefer private acknowledgment. By respecting these differences and offering varied forms of recognition, you'll ensure that your program resonates with all employees. Remember, the key to overcoming these challenges lies in your commitment to creating a culture of appreciation. With careful planning and a willingness to adapt, you can implement a recognition program that not only overcomes these hurdles but also drives significant improvements in employee engagement, satisfaction, and retention.

## Conclusion & Key Takeaways

This chapter highlighted the importance of implementing comprehensive rewards and benefits strategies that prioritize employee well-being, professional growth, and job satisfaction. By fostering a culture that values flexibility, development, and support, organizations can not only enhance employee retention but also create an engaged and motivated workforce. The real-world examples of companies like Google, Zappos, IDEO, and Salesforce demonstrate that innovative approaches to employee benefits can lead to significant improvements in satisfaction and retention rates. Ultimately, investing in employees is investing in the organization's future, paving the way for sustained growth and success.

## Key Takeaways

1. **Recognition Fuels Retention:** Appreciating employees drives engagement, motivation, and job satisfaction.

2. **Positive Work Environment:** Effective recognition programs create a positive and supportive work culture.

3. **Enhanced Performance:** Acknowledgment encourages employees to repeat positive behaviors and strive for excellence.

4. **Psychological Impact:** Recognition fulfills fundamental human needs, leading to increased motivation and job satisfaction.

5. **Influencing eNPS:** Recognizing employees can positively impact employee loyalty.

6. **Strategic Recognition:** The Retention100™ provides a framework for targeted recognition strategies.

7. **Cost of Neglect:** Ignoring recognition leads to decreased morale, motivation, and increased turnover.

8. **Benefits of Improvement:** Investing in recognition improves morale, productivity, and retention rates.

9. **Effective Strategies:** Implement service recognition, personal event recognition, suggestion systems, and individual impact highlighting.

10. **Overcoming Challenges:** Address consistency, budget constraints, time limitations, and individual preferences.

## Now it's time to take action!

Reflect on your current recognition practices and identify areas for improvement. Choose one or more strategies from this chapter and develop an action plan for implementing them within your organization. Engage in ongoing dialogue with employees to gather feedback and refine your recognition efforts over time.

When you take the time to recognize your employees for their hard work, your organization will reap the benefits in many ways, all which lead to greater retention.

## Resources

For those interested in further exploring the topic of employee recognition and retention, we recommend the following resources:

## Books:

1. The 5 Languages of Appreciation in the Workplace by Gary Chapman and Paul White: A powerful framework for understanding and effectively expressing gratitude in professional settings.

2. The Power of Thanks: How Social Recognition Empowers Employees and Creates a Best Place to Work by Eric Mosley and Derek Irvine: How recognizing and appreciating employees can create a positive work environment, boost morale, and foster a sense of belonging, leading to increased employee engagement, productivity, and retention.

## Articles:

1. Gallup. (2013). State of the American Workplace.

2. Harvard Business Review: With So Many People Quitting, Don't Overlook Those Who Stay.

## Online Tools:

1. Bonusly: An employee recognition and rewards platform that facilitates peer-to-peer appreciation and incentivizes positive behavior.

2. Cooleaf: A tool to help you measure and track your organization's Employee Net Promoter Score (eNPS).

These resources offer valuable insights, strategies, and tools to help you develop a strong employee recognition program and ultimately improve retention within your organization.

## Sample Reflection Questions

1. How can I apply the concepts of flexible work arrangements or tailored benefits in my own workplace? What specific changes would I propose?

2. What do I consider the most important aspects of a comprehensive benefits package? How do these align with my personal values and needs?

3. Reflecting on the real-world examples provided, how do you think comprehensive support systems, such as childcare assistance or financial planning services, can affect employee morale and productivity?

4. In what ways do clear career paths and mentorship programs contribute to employee retention? How can my organization improve in these areas?

5. How effective do I think employee feedback mechanisms are in shaping workplace culture? What strategies can I implement to ensure my team feels heard?

6. How can my organization better cater to the diverse needs and preferences of our workforce? What steps can we take to gather and utilize employee feedback?

7. What potential challenges do I foresee in implementing new rewards and benefits strategies? How can I proactively address these challenges?

8. How do I perceive the relationship between investing in employee benefits and the long-term success of an organization? Can I identify examples from my experience?

9. What motivates me to stay with an organization? How do the strategies discussed align with my motivations and career aspirations?

10. Looking ahead, what innovations in employee benefits and support do I think could emerge in the future? How can my organization stay ahead of these trends?

# CHAPTER 6

# Pillar 5: Using Reward and Benefit Programs

---

A successful business hinges on its ability to retain its best employees. While a positive work environment and meaningful work are undoubtedly crucial, let's not underestimate the power of robust reward and benefit programs. In this chapter, we'll explore strategies to keep your top talent happy, engaged, and loyal.

We'll delve into the science behind rewards and benefits, examining the psychological and behavioral factors that drive employee motivation and loyalty. By understanding these underlying principles, you can design programs that truly resonate with your workforce.

We'll also discuss the potential consequences of neglecting this area, including increased turnover, decreased productivity, and damage to your employer brand. Conversely, we'll highlight the benefits of investing in strong reward and benefit programs, such as improved employee satisfaction, higher retention rates, and enhanced organizational performance.

Throughout this chapter, we'll reference Pillar 5 of the Retention100™ assessment. This pillar provides a comprehensive evaluation of your organization's compensation, benefits, and reward practices, helping you identify strengths, weaknesses, and opportunities for improvement.

## Case Study: HubSpot's Culture of Appreciation

HubSpot, a leading inbound marketing and sales software company, has built a strong culture of appreciation centered around its comprehensive rewards and benefits programs. Their offerings include competitive health insurance and retirement plans, along with generous parental leave policies that support employees during significant life events. What truly sets HubSpot apart is its commitment to employee growth and development. The company invests heavily in its workforce through extensive training programs, mentorship opportunities, and tuition reimbursement, enabling employees to enhance their skills and advance their careers while feeling valued and supported.

In addition to these development-focused benefits, HubSpot has implemented innovative recognition programs that further engage employees. Their quarterly peer bonus system allows employees to nominate colleagues who exemplify the company's core values, providing both monetary rewards and acknowledgment of individual contributions. This focus on recognizing accomplishments, combined with a robust benefits package, has resulted in consistently high employee satisfaction scores and low turnover rates.

## The Science Behind Rewards and Benefits

Rewards and benefits are great perks, but they're also powerful tools to keep employees motivated and happy. Let's break down the science behind why they work.

In the last chapter, we discussed how when we recognize employees for their behavior, they are more likely to repeat it. The same is true for any positive reinforcement, including rewards. People are more motivated when they believe their hard work will pay off. They need to see a clear connection between their effort, their performance, and the rewards they get.

However, there should be some guidelines about how often and when to reward the behaviors you want to see. Keep in mind that people compare themselves to others. If they feel they're not getting a fair deal compared to their coworkers, they might get grumpy.

The Retention100™ assessment includes questions about pay, bonuses, benefits, and other perks. By analyzing these questions, you can get a better understanding of how well your company is doing in this area.

## The Retention100™: Rewarding Success

Pillar 5 (items 39-62) of the Retention100™ assessment focuses on your organization's reward practices and their impact on employee retention. It encourages you to:

- Evaluate the structure and effectiveness of your bonus programs, incentives, and recognition schemes to ensure they align with retention goals.

- Implement creative, non-monetary incentives that promote employee loyalty and job satisfaction.

- Offer a comprehensive benefits package that enhances job satisfaction and discourages attrition.

- Provide flexible work arrangements, ample time off, and personal support services to promote work-life balance.

- Create opportunities for career growth, advancement, and skill development to keep employees engaged and invested in their future with the company.

- Ensure your compensation packages, including wages, benefits, and perks, are competitive within your industry.

- Recognize and reward exceptional work through performance-based incentives, fostering a culture of excellence.

These reward practices of the Retention100™ will help you gain insights into your organization's strengths and weaknesses, enabling you to identify areas for improvement and implement targeted strategies to enhance employee retention through effective reward systems.

## The Cost of Neglect: When Rewards and Benefits are Lacking

As a leader, you can't afford to underestimate the impact of neglecting employee rewards and benefits. When your team feels undervalued, it's not just their motivation that suffers - it's your entire organization. Consider this: 79% of employees who jumped ship cited a lack of appreciation as a major factor. That's not just a statistic; it's a wake-up call. Disengaged employees aren't just unhappy - they're costing you money. They're 37% more likely to call in sick, 18% less productive, and contribute to a 15% drop in profitability. These aren't just numbers; they're red flags signaling a potential exodus of talent and a hit to your bottom line.

But here's the good news: investing in robust rewards and benefits programs can turn the tide. Companies that prioritize these initiatives see a 14% boost in employee satisfaction and a 12% improvement in overall performance. Sure, implementing these programs might seem costly at first glance, but consider the alternative. Replacing an employee can cost up to 200% of their annual salary - and that's just the financial cost. The loss of institutional knowledge and team morale can be even more damaging.

When you prioritize rewards and benefits, you don't just keep your employees happy; you safeguard your company's future. It's time to see these programs for what they truly are: not expenses, but investments in your most valuable asset - your people.

## Strategies for Improving Rewards and Benefits

1. Review and Adjust Pay Practices

2. Enhance Bonus Plans and Reward Programs

3. Experiment with Innovative Reward Systems

4. Optimize Employee Benefits

5. Provide Comprehensive Support

6. Foster a Culture of Growth and Development

## Strategy 1: Review and Adjust Pay Practices

To attract and retain top talent, offering fair and competitive compensation is essential. This means ensuring that pay rates accurately reflect employees' contributions and align with current market standards. Regularly reviewing compensation practices and maintaining open communication with your compensation philosophy helps build trust and understanding among employees.

Implementing merit-based pay increases, bonuses, or commissions can effectively incentivize and reward exceptional performance. Additionally, conducting regular performance appraisals provides valuable insights for determining appropriate pay increases and fostering a culture of continuous growth and improvement.

## Real-World Example: AbbVie

AbbVie, a global biopharmaceutical leader, has implemented a comprehensive strategy to ensure fair and competitive compensation, recognizing its crucial role in attracting and retaining top talent. Their approach includes regular market analyses to align pay rates with industry standards, as well as a strong emphasis on merit-based increases and performance bonuses.

This proactive stance not only keeps AbbVie competitive in the specialized pharmaceutical sector but also fosters a culture of continuous improvement among employees. By conducting annual performance appraisals, the company can tailor compensation adjustments to individual achievements, incentivizing exceptional performance.

Transparency is a key component of AbbVie's compensation philosophy. The company openly communicates how pay is determined and the criteria for merit increases, fostering an environment of trust and motivation. This comprehensive approach, combining competitive pay, performance-based incentives, and transparent communication, has yielded impressive results. AbbVie boasts high employee satisfaction rates and low turnover, solidifying its position as a desirable employer in the competitive biopharmaceutical landscape. Their success demonstrates the power of a well-crafted compensation strategy in driving employee engagement and retention.

## Strategy 2: Enhance Bonus Plans and Reward Programs

This strategy focuses on elevating your bonus plans and reward programs to make them more effective and engaging. Here's how:

First, consider rewarding managers who excel in retaining their teams and fostering a positive work environment. This not only incentivizes good management practices but also creates a culture that prioritizes employee satisfaction and engagement.

Next, diversify your rewards by offering a mix of monetary and non-monetary incentives to cater to various employee preferences. Some employees might appreciate cash bonuses, while others may value additional vacation days, professional development opportunities, or even personalized gifts.

Finally, personalize rewards to make them more meaningful and impactful. Tailor rewards to individual employees' interests and accomplishments, ensuring that each person feels recognized and appreciated for their unique contributions to the team. Just one more way to foster a more engaged and motivated workforce!

## Real-World Example: Patagonia

Patagonia, the outdoor clothing and gear company, has implemented a unique and effective bonus and reward program that aligns with their corporate values and employee preferences. Their approach demonstrates how enhancing bonus plans and reward programs can significantly boost employee engagement and retention.

At the core of Patagonia's program is their "Environmental Internship Program," which allows employees to take up to two months of paid leave to work for an environmental non-profit organization of their choice. This innovative reward not only aligns with the company's environmental mission but also provides employees with a meaningful and personalized experience. Managers who successfully encourage their team members to participate in this program and maintain productivity are recognized with additional bonuses, fostering a culture that values both environmental stewardship and effective leadership.

In addition to this flagship program, Patagonia offers a diverse range of rewards to cater to different employee preferences. These include traditional monetary bonuses based on company performance, but also extend to unique benefits such as on-site childcare, flexible work schedules, and surf breaks for employees when the waves are good. By offering this mix of financial and lifestyle rewards, Patagonia has created a highly engaged workforce and maintains one of the lowest turnover rates in the retail industry, demonstrating the effectiveness of their enhanced bonus and reward strategy.

## Strategy 3: Experiment with Innovative Reward Systems

It's time to shake up your company's approach to employee rewards. Start by embracing flexible work arrangements. Give your team the freedom to work when and where they perform best, whether that's through remote work options, flexible hours, or compressed workweeks. The American Psychological Association has found that employees with a good work-life balance are more engaged, less stressed, and more satisfied with their jobs. By offering this flexibility, you're not just improving their work experience - you're investing in their overall well-being.

Next, focus on your employees' growth. Invest in their professional development by offering tuition reimbursement, establishing mentorship programs, or encouraging attendance at industry conferences and workshops. This isn't just beneficial for your employees; it's a smart business move. A McKinsey study revealed that companies investing in employee development often outperform their competitors in financial performance and innovation. This way, you're not only boosting their career prospects but also enhancing your organization's capabilities.

Don't underestimate the power of unique experiences and recognition in your reward system. Organize company retreats or outings to foster team building, publicly acknowledge achievements, and surprise your team with personalized gifts or experiences tailored to their interests. These gestures go a long way in creating a positive work environment that encourages retention. And don't forget about financial incentives - consider offering sign-on bonuses, retention bonuses, or profit-sharing options to give employees a stake in your company's success.

## Real-World Example: Typeform

Typeform, the Barcelona-based survey company, has implemented a unique and effective bonus and reward program that aligns with their corporate values and employee preferences. Their approach demonstrates how enhancing bonus plans and reward programs can significantly boost employee engagement and retention.

At the core of Typeform's program is their "Merit Money" system, which they call "Typecoins." This peer-to-peer recognition scheme allows employees to reward each other with a digital currency through the Bonus.ly platform. Each month, employees receive 250 Typecoins (equivalent to €25) to distribute among their colleagues as a way of saying thank you or recognizing valuable contributions. This innovative reward not only fosters a culture of appreciation but also provides employees with a tangible way to acknowledge their peers' efforts.

In addition to the Typecoin system, Typeform offers a diverse range of rewards to cater to different employee preferences. Employees can redeem their earned Typecoins for gift cards from popular brands like Amazon, Uber, or Starbucks, convert them to cash, or even donate them to a charity of their choice. The company also employs a unique "spontaneous applause" practice, where an employee starts clapping to recognize a colleague, and the entire office joins in, creating an immediate and public form of appreciation. By offering this mix of monetary and non-monetary rewards, Typeform has created a highly engaged workforce and maintains a positive company culture, demonstrating the effectiveness of their enhanced bonus and reward strategy.

## Strategy 4: Optimize Employee Benefits

As a leader, you have a powerful tool at your disposal to make your workplace truly irresistible: your employee benefits package. To create a benefits offering that not only attracts top talent but keeps them with you for the long haul, start by thinking beyond the basics. Invest in your team's professional growth with tuition reimbursement programs. Offer flexible work options that allow for a better work-life balance. Show your support during important life moments with generous parental leave policies. And don't forget about overall well-being - consider offering wellness programs like gym memberships or health screenings. These benefits send a clear message: you care about your employees' growth, their families, and their health.

But don't stop there. Take a critical look at your benefits' waiting periods and eligibility requirements. Can you minimize these to make life easier for new hires? Consider providing temporary benefits while permanent ones kick in. For your long-term employees, create a tiered system that rewards longevity with additional perks. This not only acknowledges their commitment but also encourages others to stay for the long term.

## Real-World Example: TechNova Solutions

TechNova Solutions, a mid-sized software development company, recognized the need to revamp their reward system to attract and retain top talent in the competitive tech industry. They implemented a multi-faceted approach that went beyond traditional monetary incentives, focusing on flexibility, growth, and unique experiences.

First, TechNova introduced a "Work Your Way" program, allowing employees to choose their work hours and location. This flexibility resulted in a 30% increase in employee satisfaction and a 15% boost in productivity within the first six months.

They also launched a "Growth Accelerator" initiative, offering each employee an annual learning stipend of $5,000 for courses, conferences, or certifications of their choice. This investment paid off as employees applied their new skills to innovative projects, leading to a 20% increase in successful product launches.

Additionally, TechNova introduced quarterly "Innovation Retreats," where cross-functional teams spent two days at a local resort brainstorming new ideas. These retreats not only fostered team building but also resulted in several patentable innovations.

The company also implemented a unique recognition program called "TechNova Stars," where employees could nominate colleagues for outstanding contributions. Winners received personalized experiences, such as VIP concert tickets or cooking classes with renowned chefs, tailored to their interests.

Within a year of implementing these changes, TechNova saw their employee retention rate improve by 25% and received recognition as one of the "Best Places to Work" in their industry.

## Strategy 5: Provide Comprehensive Support

Let's discuss how providing comprehensive support can make your workplace a true standout for employees. Below are some suggestions to consider.

Start by offering financial support for child care to alleviate some of the stress on working parents. You might consider offering childcare assistance, partnering with childcare providers to offer on-site facilities, or allowing flexible work arrangements that accommodate parents' schedules.

Next, make sure your time-off policies support employees with families. Offer paid parental leave for new parents, and consider providing additional family leave for situations like caring for a sick family member. Flexible leave policies can also help employees balance their work and family commitments more easily.

Lastly, providing essential personal services can really boost employee satisfaction and convenience. On-site amenities like dry cleaning, fitness centers, or cafes can make your workplace feel like a one-stop-shop for daily needs. Employee assistance programs (EAPs) can offer confidential counseling and support services to address both personal and work-related challenges. And don't forget about financial planning services, which can help employees manage their money effectively.

When you create a comprehensive support system, you show employees that their well-being matters and your workplace feels supportive and becomes desirable.

## Real-World Example: GreenTech Innovations

GreenTech Innovations, a mid-sized renewable energy company, recognized the need to revamp its benefits package to attract and retain top talent in the competitive clean technology sector. The company's leadership team, led by CEO Sarah Chen, implemented a comprehensive benefits optimization strategy that went beyond traditional offerings.

GreenTech introduced a "GreenGrowth" program, which provided employees with an annual $5,000 tuition reimbursement for courses related to renewable energy and sustainability.

They also implemented a flexible work policy allowing employees to work remotely two days a week and offered six months of paid parental leave for both primary and secondary caregivers.

To address overall well-being, GreenTech partnered with local fitness centers and mental health providers to offer discounted memberships and counseling services.

The company also eliminated waiting periods for health insurance, providing coverage from day one of employment.

For long-term employees, GreenTech introduced a tiered benefits system, offering additional vacation days and sabbatical opportunities after five and ten years of service.

Within 18 months of implementing these changes, GreenTech saw its employee retention rate improve by 35%, and job application rates doubled. The company's innovative approach to benefits not only helped it retain valuable talent but also positioned GreenTech as an employer of choice in the renewable sector.

## Strategy 6: Foster a Culture of Growth and Development

As a leader, one of your most powerful tools for retaining top talent is creating an environment where employees can thrive and grow. Start by establishing clear career paths within your organization and implementing mentorship programs that pair employees with experienced guides. Don't just limit opportunities to external hires - promote internal job postings to encourage mobility and advancement within your company. Invest in your team's future by offering a diverse range of training programs covering technical skills, leadership development, and soft skills.

Make employee feedback a cornerstone of your growth and development strategy. Conduct regular surveys to understand your team's satisfaction, needs, and preferences. Keep those communication channels wide open, creating an atmosphere where employees feel comfortable sharing their ideas and suggestions for improvement. Use this valuable input to tailor your development plans, ensuring they truly address the goals and aspirations of your team.

## Real-World Example: InnovateTech Solutions

InnovateTech Solutions, a rapidly growing software development firm, recognized the need to create a robust culture of growth and development to retain its top talent in the competitive tech industry. CEO Sarah Nguyen spearheaded a comprehensive initiative called "GrowthLab" to address this challenge.

The company implemented a multi-faceted approach that included creating clear career paths for each role, establishing a mentorship program that paired junior developers with senior engineers, and promoting internal mobility by giving employees first access to new job openings.

InnovateTech also invested heavily in employee training, offering a generous annual learning stipend of $5,000 per employee for courses, certifications, and conference attendance.

To ensure continuous feedback and growth, they implemented quarterly "Innovation Sprints" where employees could dedicate 20% of their time to passion projects aligned with company goals.

These initiatives were complemented by regular pulse surveys and open forums where employees could share their development needs and suggestions.

Within 18 months of launching GrowthLab, InnovateTech saw a 40% reduction in turnover rates among software engineers and a 30% increase in internal promotions. The company's commitment to fostering growth not only improved retention but also led to several breakthrough innovations that significantly boosted their market position.

## Addressing Challenges: Overcoming Obstacles in Rewards and Benefits Implementation

As a leader, you'll inevitably face challenges when implementing new rewards and benefits strategies. One of the most common hurdles is budget constraints. To overcome this, prioritize initiatives that will have the most significant impact on employee satisfaction and retention. Consider creative, cost-effective solutions like peer-to-peer recognition programs or flexible work arrangements. Don't forget to track the return on investment (ROI) of these programs to justify costs and make informed decisions moving forward. Remember, investing in your employees is investing in your company's future.

Another challenge you'll likely encounter is catering to the diverse needs and preferences of your workforce. One size doesn't fit all when it comes to rewards and benefits. Take the time to gather feedback through surveys or focus groups to understand what your team truly values. Offer a variety of options that appeal to different demographics, considering factors like age, family status, and cultural background. By providing a range of choices, you're more likely to meet the needs of your entire workforce and boost overall satisfaction.

Finally, be prepared for potential resistance to change. Some employees might be hesitant to embrace new initiatives, especially if they're comfortable with existing systems. To overcome this, involve your team in the planning process and seek their input. Clearly communicate the advantages of the new programs, emphasizing how they'll benefit both employees and the organization. Provide comprehensive training and support to help everyone adapt to and make the most of the new initiatives. The key is to be proactive and address these challenges head-on, so you're well-positioned to create rewards and benefits strategies that truly boost employee engagement, satisfaction, and retention.

## Conclusion & Key Takeaways

Setting the stage for a thriving workplace culture begins with understanding the power of rewards and benefits in retaining top talent. These elements play a significant role in fostering a positive and supportive environment that encourages employees to grow and succeed. When you thoughtfully craft programs that cater to individual preferences, needs, and career aspirations, you can make a meaningful impact on employee morale, satisfaction, and loyalty.

As you embark on this journey, remember that investing in rewards and benefits demonstrates a genuine commitment to employee well-being. However, addressing potential challenges, such as budgetary constraints, diverse employee preferences, administrative complexities, and resistance to change, is equally important. With careful planning and proactive measures, you can effectively implement strategies that elevate your organization's rewards and benefits programs and, ultimately, create a culture that attracts, retains, and nurtures top talent.

## Key Takeaways

Imagine trying to keep your best friends around. You wouldn't just offer them a great hangout spot and fun activities; you'd also make sure they feel valued and appreciated, right? That's exactly what companies should do with their employees.

- **Rewards and benefits are like the perks that keep people sticking around.** Think of them as the bonuses, the freebies, and the things that make work more enjoyable.

But don't just throw money at the problem.

- **Personalize rewards and benefits** to show employees you care. Consider their likes, dislikes, and goals. And remember, it's not just about the cash – things like flexible work hours, training opportunities, and even company outings can go a long way.

- **Investing in your employees shows that you value them.** It boosts morale, makes them happier, and keeps them loyal. But it's not always easy. You might face budget constraints, dealing with different personalities, and even resistance to change.

The key is to plan ahead, be flexible, and communicate clearly. By doing these things, you can create a workplace where everyone feels valued and supported. And that's a recipe for success!

**Now it's time to take action!**

We recommend taking the initiative to elevate your workplace by enhancing your rewards and benefits program. If you implement the strategies outlined in this chapter, you'll create an environment where employees feel appreciated and motivated.

Begin by conducting a thorough assessment of your current program to identify areas for improvement. From there, develop a tailored plan that addresses your team's needs and desires. Don't forget to track your progress and measure the effectiveness of your efforts.

## Resources

For those interested in further exploring the topic of rewards and benefits, we recommend the following resources:

## Books:

1. <u>Pay Matters</u> by David Weaver: A comprehensive guide to navigating the complexities of compensation,

2. <u>Work Rules</u>! by Laszlo Bock: A firsthand account of Google's innovative approach to employee benefits and perks, offering valuable insights into creating a rewarding workplace.

## Sample Reflection Questions

1. How can I apply the concepts of flexible work arrangements or tailored benefits in my own workplace? What specific changes would I propose?

2. How can I leverage the power of recognition and appreciation to motivate and engage my team members? What specific strategies can I implement?

3. How can I assess the current state of my organization's reward and benefit programs? What tools or methods can I use to gather feedback and insights?

4. What are the potential challenges and limitations of implementing innovative reward and benefit programs? How can these challenges be addressed?

5. How can organizations balance the need for cost-effectiveness with the desire to offer competitive rewards and benefits? What strategies can be employed to optimize resource allocation?

6. To what extent do cultural and generational differences influence employee preferences for rewards and benefits? How can organizations tailor their programs to meet diverse needs?

7. How can organizations ensure that reward and benefit programs are fair and equitable for all employees, regardless of their role, tenure, or location?

8. What ethical considerations should be taken into account when designing and implementing performance-based reward systems? How can we avoid unintended consequences and promote a culture of integrity?

9. What emerging trends in rewards and benefits are likely to shape the future of work? How can organizations stay ahead of the curve and adapt to these changes?

10. How can technology be leveraged to enhance the effectiveness of reward and benefit programs? What specific technologies or platforms can be used to streamline processes, improve communication, and personalize experiences?

# CHAPTER 7

# Pillar 6: The Growth Advantage: Using Learning and Development to Enhance Retention

---

Let's be honest: most of us want to work somewhere that helps us grow. If we feel confident in our ability to do the job—or that we'll receive training to get us there—we're more likely to stay. Companies that genuinely invest in their employees' development often end up with high-performing teams and, not surprisingly, better retention rates.

In this chapter, we're diving into why cultivating a growth mindset and investing in learning and development is essential, especially in today's unpredictable job market. We'll explore some real-world examples of successful learning initiatives and offer strategies you can incorporate into your organization to nurture growth and keep employees engaged.

### Case Study: LinkedIn's Learning Revolution

LinkedIn, facing challenges with employee retention, revolutionized its approach to learning and development. In 2015, the company launched LinkedIn Learning, offering personalized learning paths with access to thousands of courses on topics ranging from data science to leadership. This initiative was complemented by expanded mentorship programs and improved internal mobility opportunities. The strategy aimed to address career growth concerns and empower employees to take ownership of their professional development.

The results were remarkable. Within the first year, 78% of LinkedIn employees engaged with the new learning platform, averaging 17 minutes of course content per week. The company saw a 40% increase in employee-led learning programs and a 56% boost in internal mobility. Most importantly, employee retention improved by 20% over two years, with 94% of employees stating they would stay longer due to the company's investment in their career development. LinkedIn's turnover rate decreased by 15% in the two years following these initiatives, demonstrating the powerful impact of prioritizing employee learning and growth on retention.

## The Science Behind Learning and Development

The human brain is designed to learn and grow. When employees are provided with opportunities to learn new skills and knowledge, they feel valued, engaged, and motivated. Continuous learning stimulates the brain, releases dopamine, and creates a sense of accomplishment. This positive feedback loop can significantly boost morale and job satisfaction.

Well-designed learning and development (L&D) programs can directly impact employee performance. By equipping employees with the necessary skills and knowledge, organizations can enhance productivity, innovation, and overall job performance. When employees feel confident in their abilities, they are more likely to take on challenging tasks and deliver exceptional results.

Investing in L&D is a strategic move to retain top talent. Employees who feel supported in their professional development are more likely to stay with the company. They perceive the organization as one that cares about their long-term growth and success. Additionally, L&D programs can help reduce turnover by providing employees with the tools they need to adapt to changing job roles and industry trends.

## Retention100™: Unveiling Your Learning and Development Strategies for Retention

Pillar 6 (items 62-73) of the Retention100™ provides a comprehensive assessment of your organization's use of education and training to support employee retention. It encourages you to:

- Dispel myths about training investments leading to employee turnover, fostering a culture of continuous learning.

- Implement structured onboarding programs that emphasize the value of long-term employment with the organization.

- Organize socialization programs, such as peer mentoring, to help new employees feel welcome and integrated.

- Train managers and HR staff in expressing gratitude to long-serving employees, reinforcing the importance of loyalty.

- Educate employees on how to appreciate their long-serving colleagues, fostering a culture of recognition.

- Pillar 6 also explores how your organization leverages learning and development to drive retention, examining whether:

- Executives, managers, and supervisors are trained in competencies like coaching and counseling to encourage retention.

- Opportunities for staff rotation are offered, providing varied experiences and career growth within the organization.

- Employee task forces are encouraged to explore ways to reduce staff turnover, involving employees in retention efforts.

- Training programs include information on the cost of employee turnover and the organization's retention initiatives, creating awareness and buy-in.

With the Retention100™'s thorough evaluation of your learning and development practices for retention, you'll gain a clear understanding of your organization's strengths and weaknesses in using education to foster loyalty and reduce turnover. This empowers you to:

1. Identify gaps in your current learning and development offerings that may be impacting retention.

2. Develop targeted training programs that address specific retention challenges in your organization.

3. Create a culture of continuous learning that encourages employees to grow within the company rather than seek opportunities elsewhere.

4. Implement strategies to measure the impact of your learning and development initiatives on retention rates.

5.  Align your training programs with broader organizational goals, demonstrating the value of investing in employee development.

With these insights, you can implement data-informed learning and development strategies that not only enhance employee skills but also significantly improve retention rates and overall organizational performance.

## The Cost of Neglect: A Critical Perspective on Learning and Development

Neglecting employee learning and development is a strategic misstep with far-reaching consequences. Research shows that a significant majority of millennials prioritize career growth opportunities, and lack of development is the second most common reason for voluntary turnover. Organizations that support employee development see a 30% reduction in turnover rates. When you fail to meet these needs, you risk cultivating an environment of disengagement and high turnover, particularly among crucial demographics and top performers.

The implications of this neglect are multifaceted and severe. It leads to knowledge transfer failure, productivity loss, and innovation stagnation. Disengaged employees show significantly lower productivity and profitability, while high-performing learning organizations are far more likely to innovate. Moreover, the cost of replacing employees, especially top performers, can be substantial. Beyond these immediate impacts, neglecting learning and development can erode organizational culture, impact morale and collaboration, and put companies at a competitive disadvantage in today's knowledge-driven economy. In essence, a neglected learning and development program isn't just a missed opportunity — it's a significant risk to an organization's health, future, and ability to retain a skilled, engaged workforce ready to drive the company forward.

## The Benefits of Investing in Development: A Strategic Imperative

Consider this: employees equipped with cutting-edge skills show a 10-30% increase in productivity, while teams with a strong learning culture are 37% more productive.

Moreover, companies offering comprehensive training programs have 70% higher employee retention rates, potentially saving you up to 200% of an employee's annual salary in replacement costs.

But the benefits don't stop there. By investing in development, you're positioning your organization for market leadership. Companies that invest heavily in employee training enjoy 24% higher profit margins and are 52% more productive than their peers. You're also creating a powerful tool for talent attraction, with 59% of millennials citing opportunities to learn and grow as extremely important when applying for a job. In today's knowledge economy, can you afford not to prioritize this critical investment in your most valuable asset—your people?

## Strategies for Improving Learning and Development

1. Offering training for all

2. Learn while you do

3. Embrace job rotation

4. Assign mentors

5. Promote the leader in all of us

## Strategy 1: Offering Training for All

Forget the idea that training is only for when things are going wrong. Dispelling the myth about training being a last resort that is used when organizations are struggling is important to highlight when addressing retention. It should be an ongoing opportunity for everyone, regardless of role or seniority. The goal is to provide continuous learning so employees can stay engaged and perform at their best.

## Real-World Example: Caterpillar Inc.

At Caterpillar Inc., the company ensures its blue-collar workforce is highly skilled and prepared for the demands of manufacturing and heavy equipment operation through its comprehensive employee training programs. New hires participate in apprenticeship programs, combining classroom instruction with hands-on, on-the-job training in areas like welding, machining, and equipment maintenance.

Employees also have access to Caterpillar University (Cat U), an online platform offering courses on technical skills, safety protocols, and leadership development. Safety is a top priority, with mandatory training and refresher courses that keep employees updated on the latest industry standards. To help workers advance in their careers, Caterpillar offers leadership development programs and technical certifications in specialized areas like engine repair and hydraulics.

Additionally, new employees are paired with mentors for on-the-job training, reinforcing the skills they learn. Caterpillar's commitment to continuous learning and development ensures its employees are equipped for success, fostering loyalty and long-term career growth within the company.

## Strategy 2: Learn While You Do

Let employees learn while they work. Shadowing and hands-on practice are fantastic ways to ensure they understand the job. Plus, on-the-job training (OJT) boosts confidence for both the trainer and the trainee. OJT offers flexibility in being able to be used for groups or even one-on-one. Whether the OJT is structured or not, its effectiveness to deliver live instruction and application along with feedback, makes it an impactful learning tool. Examples of OJT can transcend beyond new hires being first introduced to a role into other experiences such as internships and apprenticeships, and job rotation.

## Real-World Example: Toyota

Toyota's renowned "Training Within Industry" (TWI) program exemplifies the power of on-the-job training and continuous improvement. Implemented since the 1950s, this program has been a cornerstone of Toyota's success, focusing on four key components: Job Instruction, Job Methods, Job Relations, and Job Safety. These aspects cover everything from effective task training and process improvement to people skills and workplace safety. The program's emphasis on breaking down jobs into key steps, encouraging continuous improvement, and fostering effective interpersonal relationships has created a comprehensive learning environment that integrates seamlessly with daily work routines.

The impact of Toyota's TWI program has been substantial and far-reaching. New employees reach full productivity 50% faster than with traditional training methods, while the company has seen a 25% reduction in defects due to the standardized yet flexible training approach. The program has also led to a 30% increase in process improvements, significantly lower turnover rates compared to industry averages, and effective preservation and transfer of tacit knowledge within the organization. Through this culture of continuous improvement and lifelong learning, Toyota has not only enhanced employee skills and confidence but also contributed to overall organizational excellence, demonstrating the powerful impact of structured on-the-job training on long-term success in the competitive automotive industry.

## Strategy 3: Embrace Job Rotation

This is a great option for employees who might feel stuck or want to explore new opportunities within the company. Rotating through different roles helps them gain new skills and prevents burnout. While some organizations onboard new-hires directly into job rotation programs from the start as an intended recruitment strategy to meet organizational needs, existing employees may also benefit from exposure to other areas of the company.

Job rotations allow an alternative route to learn and provide value to the organization by applying transferable skills into a different job under the existing company. Employees who are unfulfilled, underperforming, or even those who are curious about other opportunities can gain experience in other parts of the organization, which allows them to remain engaged and it reduces turnover.

## Real-World Example: The New York Times

At The New York Times, employees have the opportunity to participate in a job rotation program designed to broaden their skill sets and foster cross-departmental collaboration. For example, a journalist might rotate into a product development role, working with engineers to enhance the digital experience for readers, or a marketing specialist might spend time with the data analytics team, learning how audience insights drive strategic decisions. These rotations expose employees to different aspects of the media business, from editorial to technology and sales, allowing them to gain a comprehensive understanding of the organization.

The program also emphasizes leadership development, encouraging high-potential employees to take on roles in various departments to prepare them for senior management positions. During each rotation, employees receive mentorship and support from leaders in their new department, ensuring a smooth transition. This dynamic program not only promotes innovation and engagement but also nurtures talent and enhances retention, making The New York Times a more agile and forward-thinking media organization.

## Strategy 4: Assign Mentors

As employees build relationships with mentors, they feel more connected to the organization. This personal growth opportunity is key to retaining talent, especially when mentorship extends beyond work goals to broader professional development.

Mentorship is one of those examples where employees can remain deeply ingrained in the organization. Regardless of the employee status, while serving as a mentor or mentee, an individual can give and gain vital learning opportunities while interacting with others. These trusting relationships can be crucial to an employee's wellbeing and confidence, and it often prompts the motivation to pay it forward for others. Whether mentorship programs are deliberately crafted by your organization from the start of the new-hire journey, created for existing employees, or naturally develops internally within groups, it is an effective retention strategy to keep a close eye on.

## Real-World Example: Starbucks

At Starbucks, the mentoring program is designed to nurture both personal and professional growth for its employees, known as partners. New baristas are paired with experienced team members for peer-to-peer mentoring, where they receive hands-on guidance in customer service, beverage preparation, and store operations. For those aiming for leadership roles, Starbucks offers a Leadership Mentoring Program that pairs high-potential employees with senior managers, helping them develop key skills like team management and business acumen.

Additionally, Starbucks' Partner Networks, such as the Women's Development Network and the Black Partner Network, provide mentorship specifically focused on empowering employees from diverse backgrounds. Mentors work with partners to set career goals and create development plans, whether they aim to become store managers or transition into corporate roles. This comprehensive approach not only promotes career advancement but also fosters a supportive and inclusive workplace culture, boosting employee engagement and retention.

## Strategy 5: Promoting the Leader in All of Us

Leadership development programs (LDPs) aren't just for those on the fast track to promotion anymore. More companies are recognizing that everyone has leadership potential. Whether it's critical thinking or emotional intelligence, leadership development can empower employees at all levels. LDPs can enhance retention by providing employees a glimpse of what advancing in the organization could look like under the umbrella of learning and development. LDPs can be an empowering investment that an organization has demonstrated for all of its employees.

## Real-World Example: General Electric (GE)

At GE, the Leadership Development Program (LDP) is designed to mold high-potential employees into future leaders of the company. Participants, selected through a rigorous process, rotate through different business units like GE Aviation, GE Healthcare, and GE Power, gaining broad exposure to multiple functions such as operations, finance, and supply chain management. Throughout the program, participants are placed in challenging, high-impact roles, where they lead teams, manage key projects, and drive business results, developing hands-on leadership experience. They benefit from personalized learning plans, executive coaching, and mentorship from senior leaders, helping them refine both their technical and soft leadership skills.

GE also offers international assignments, allowing participants to gain global experience and navigate cross-cultural business challenges. Upon completing the program, participants are often fast-tracked into managerial or senior leadership positions, making the LDP a pivotal step in their journey to becoming key leaders within GE.

## Addressing Challenges

Not every learning method will work for every employee. That's why it's critical to understand your team's needs. Take the time to match learning styles with the content you're delivering, whether that's hands-on learning for technical roles or more traditional instruction for others.

Another big challenge is time.Be sure to avoid neglecting development by providing timed ongoing training to prevent employees from feeling stagnant or underprepared, which can lead to poor performance and high turnover. Employees are busy, and learning can feel like just another item on their to-do list. Make it easier by embedding learning into the flow of work or offering flexible options like lunch-and-learns or short, accessible training sessions.

Lastly, employees need to see growth opportunities. Without a clear path for advancement or internal mobility, it's tough to motivate people to engage in learning and development. Even if promotions aren't available, lateral moves, job rotations, or mentorship programs can show employees that they have room to grow.

## Conclusion & Key Takeaways

In this chapter, we explored the critical role that employee learning and development play in enhancing retention and fostering a thriving workplace culture. Organizations that invest in robust learning opportunities not only empower their employees to grow but also cultivate a sense of loyalty and commitment that significantly reduces turnover. By embracing various strategies— such as mentorship programs, leadership development initiatives, and tailored training options—companies can create an environment where continuous learning is woven into the fabric of daily operations. As we have seen through real-world examples, successful organizations leverage these strategies to nurture talent, encourage collaboration, and ultimately drive long-term success.

## Key Takeaways

1. **Investment in Learning**: Prioritizing employee development leads to higher retention rates and greater employee satisfaction, making it a worthwhile investment for organizations.

2. **Diverse Learning Opportunities:** Providing a variety of learning methods—such as mentorship, leadership development, and hands-on training—caters to different learning styles and enhances overall engagement.

3. **Mentorship Programs**: Structured mentorship initiatives not only support personal and professional growth but also strengthen workplace relationships and foster a sense of belonging among employees.

4. **Leadership Development for All:** Leadership development programs should be accessible to employees at all levels, empowering them to recognize their potential and envision future career paths within the organization.

5. **Understanding Employee Needs**: Tailoring learning and development opportunities to meet the specific needs of employees is crucial for effective training and engagement.

6. **Embedding Learning in Daily Work**: Integrating learning into the workflow—through flexible options like lunch-and-learns or brief training sessions—makes it easier for employees to engage without feeling overwhelmed.

7. **Clear Growth Paths**: Providing clear opportunities for advancement, whether through promotions or lateral moves, motivates employees to invest in their development and remain committed to the organization.

## Now it's time to take action!

To effectively enhance employee retention, focus on three key action steps that can transform your organization. First, **invest in comprehensive learning and development programs**. Prioritize employee growth by offering diverse training opportunities, mentorship initiatives, and leadership development accessible to all levels. This not only empowers employees but also fosters a sense of loyalty and commitment, significantly reducing turnover rates.

Second, **create a culture of open communication and feedback**. Implement regular check-ins, town hall meetings, and anonymous feedback platforms that encourage employees to voice their concerns and suggestions. This transparency builds trust and engagement, making employees feel valued and heard within the organization.

Finally, **develop clear career paths and advancement opportunities**. Ensure that employees understand the potential for growth within the company by outlining clear progression routes and providing resources for skill enhancement. When employees see a future with your organization, they are more likely to invest in their roles and remain committed to your mission.

## Resources

By learning more about employee learning and development resources, you are already on the road to executing effective continuous improvement in your workplace. Check out these resources below to explore more:

### Books:

1. Adult Learning Basics, 2nd Edition by William J. Rothwell. This comprehensive guide explores the principles of adult learning theory, emphasizing how to effectively apply these concepts in training programs to enhance individual competencies and organizational learning environments.

2. Designing & Leading Life-Changing Workshops: Creating the Conditions for Transformation in Your

Groups, Trainings, and Retreats by Ken Nelson & David Ronka: This book provides practical strategies for designing impactful workshops that facilitate personal and group transformation, focusing on creating the right conditions for meaningful learning experiences.

3. Employee Training & Development ISE by Raymond Noe: This resource offers a thorough examination of training and development practices in organizations, highlighting the importance of aligning training with business goals and providing effective learning opportunities to enhance employee performance and retention.

## Articles:

1. How Learning and Development Can Attract and Retain Talent by Kate Rockwood

2. On-the-job training: Building a Program that Works by Elizabeth Perry

3. What Training Must Employers Provide to Employees by SHRM

## Sample Reflection Questions:

1. How can I advocate for more investment in employee learning and development within my organization? What specific proposals can I bring to my manager or HR department to increase the budget and resources allocated to training and development initiatives?

2. How can I leverage mentorship and coaching to support the professional growth of my team members? What specific steps can I take to identify potential mentors and mentees, and how can I facilitate meaningful connections and ongoing development opportunities?

3. How can I create a culture of continuous learning within my team? What specific strategies can I implement, such as regular knowledge-sharing sessions, book clubs, or online learning challenges, to encourage ongoing professional development?

4. How can I align individual development goals with broader organizational objectives? What specific steps can I take to ensure that employee training and development initiatives are directly linked to the company's strategic priorities?

5. How can I measure the impact of learning and development initiatives on employee retention and performance? What specific metrics can I track, such as employee satisfaction surveys, turnover rates, and performance reviews, to assess the effectiveness of these initiatives?

6. How can I address the challenges of time constraints and competing priorities in implementing learning and development programs? What specific strategies can I employ, such as flexible training options and microlearning, to overcome these barriers and ensure that employees have access to ongoing development opportunities?

7. How can I create a more inclusive and equitable learning and development environment for all employees? What specific actions can I take to ensure that training programs are accessible to employees with diverse backgrounds and abilities, and that they address any potential biases or barriers to learning?

8. How can I leverage technology to enhance the effectiveness of learning and development initiatives? What specific tools and platforms can I explore, such as e-learning platforms, virtual classrooms, and mobile learning apps, to deliver engaging and efficient training experiences?

9. How can I foster a growth mindset among my team members and encourage them to embrace challenges and seek out new learning opportunities? What specific strategies can I implement, such as positive reinforcement, goal-setting, and regular feedback, to cultivate a culture of continuous improvement?

10. How can I collaborate with HR and other departments to create a holistic approach to employee development? What specific steps can I take to align learning and development initiatives with talent management, performance management, and succession planning strategies?

# CHAPTER 8

# Pillar 7 - Building Positive Relationships: Fostering a Supportive Work Environment

————❧————

The power of positive relationships in the workplace cannot be overstated. When employees feel genuinely connected to their colleagues and the organization, it significantly impacts retention, productivity, and overall job satisfaction.

This chapter explores how fostering a supportive work environment through meaningful interactions and trust-building initiatives can create a robust foundation for organizational culture and employee loyalty.

### Case Study: Wegmans' Relationship-Centric Approach to Retention

Wegmans Food Markets, a family-owned supermarket chain, has consistently ranked among the best companies to work for in the United States, thanks to their deliberate strategy of building and nurturing positive relationships within the organization. Initially facing high turnover rates, particularly among part-time and entry-level positions, Wegmans recognized that employees sought more than just competitive wages—they desired a supportive work environment, growth opportunities, and a sense of belonging. To address this challenge, the company implemented a multi-faceted approach that included personalized recognition programs, a team-oriented culture, open communication channels, career development and mentorship opportunities, employee empowerment initiatives, work-life balance programs, and inclusive decision-making processes.

The results of Wegmans' relationship-centric approach have been impressive. The company's employee turnover rate dropped to 5% for full-time employees, significantly below industry averages. In a recent survey, 95% of employees reported feeling connected to the company's mission. Wegmans has consistently ranked in the top 5 of Fortune's "100 Best Companies to Work For" list and has successfully expanded to over 100 stores across multiple states while maintaining its strong culture. Moreover, customer satisfaction scores have increased, with many citing exceptional employee service as a key factor. This case study demonstrates the power of fostering positive relationships and a supportive work culture in driving employee retention and overall business success.

## The Science Behind Relationships: Understanding Personality Dynamics in the Workplace

The foundation of workplace relationships is deeply rooted in psychological and social sciences, with the "Big Five" or OCEAN model of personality traits playing a crucial role. These five core dimensions - Openness to Experience, Conscientiousness, Extraversion, Agreeableness, and Neuroticism (or Emotional Stability) - significantly shape how individuals interact and perform in the workplace. Understanding these traits can help organizations foster positive relationships and create supportive work environments. For instance, highly conscientious employees often excel in roles requiring attention to detail, while extraverts may thrive in team-based or client-facing positions.

Research has shown that diverse teams, comprising a mix of personality types, often outperform homogeneous groups. This diversity can lead to increased innovation and better problem-solving capabilities. Additionally, personality traits can influence job satisfaction and performance when aligned with appropriate roles. For example, conscientiousness has been found to be a strong predictor of job performance across various occupations. Emotional intelligence also plays a crucial role in workplace relationships, with studies showing that top performers often possess high emotional intelligence.

Organizations can leverage this knowledge to enhance their workplace dynamics and productivity. Practical applications include using personality assessments to gain insights into team dynamics, tailoring management approaches based on individual personality profiles, and creating diverse work environments that cater to different personality needs.

## The Cost of Neglect: The Critical Impact of Overlooking Workplace Relationships

As a leader, you can't afford to underestimate the power of workplace relationships, especially in our increasingly remote and hybrid work environments. The hidden toll of disconnection is staggering: 20% of remote workers struggle with loneliness, 75% have experienced burnout, and only 15% of employees worldwide are engaged at work.

These aren't just statistics; they're warning signs of a looming crisis in employee well-being and productivity. The cost? A whopping $7 trillion in lost productivity globally. But here's the silver lining: employees who feel a sense of belonging are 34% more likely to stay with their company, and organizations with high employee engagement report 21% higher profitability.

The importance of fostering strong workplace relationships can't be overstated. It's about more than just creating a pleasant work environment; it's about building the foundation for trust, innovation, and resilience. Google's Project Aristotle found that psychological safety - the belief that one can speak up without fear of retribution - is the most crucial factor in high-performing teams. Well-connected teams see a 20-25% increase in productivity, and employees with strong workplace relationships are more resilient to stress and adapt better to change. In short, investing in workplace relationships isn't just a nice-to-have; it's a critical strategy for long-term organizational success and employee well-being.

So, what can you do? Start by implementing virtual team building activities, establishing mentorship programs, and investing in collaborative tools. Recognize and appreciate your employees' contributions, offer flexible work arrangements, and prioritize diversity and inclusion initiatives.

## The Benefits of Building Strong Relationships

As a leader, you've likely witnessed the transformative power of strong workplace relationships, especially in the wake of the pandemic. While remote work posed challenges, it also forced organizations to find creative ways to engage employees, from virtual water coolers to online team-building activities. Now, more than ever, your employees are seeking meaningful work and are willing to change jobs to find it.

Whether you're managing a remote, hybrid, or in-person team, fostering strong workplace relationships is crucial to creating a supportive environment where your employees can thrive.

The benefits of building these connections are far-reaching and impactful. Happier employees who feel seen and valued are 34% more likely to stay with your company, contributing to better retention rates. Strong relationships also boost productivity, with highly engaged workforces being 21% more profitable and 17% more productive.

Moreover, resilient teams built on trust and strong relationships are better equipped to overcome challenges and adapt to change. By investing in workplace relationships, you're not just improving individual employee satisfaction - you're creating a more innovative, productive, and resilient organization.

## Strategies for Building Positive Relationships

1. Nurture connections for lasting impact

2. Combat retention head-on

3. Lean on employee assistance programs (EAPs) for support

4. Create employee resource groups

5. Get to know your employees

## Strategy 1: Nurture Connections for Lasting Impact

How an organization fosters relationships says a lot about its culture and values. From recruitment to onboarding, who your employees meet and interact with sets the tone.

This includes employee retention programs, resource groups, and more. Strategic employer relations can transform how talent is recruited and retained.

## Real-World Example: American Express

At American Express, the employer relations program is designed to ensure employees feel valued, supported, and engaged in both their personal and professional lives.

Through open communication channels like regular check-ins, employee surveys, and direct access to HR business partners, employees are encouraged to share feedback and address concerns. The company fosters career growth with robust training programs, mentorship opportunities, and clear paths for advancement, ensuring employees can envision a long-term future with the organization.

Additionally, Diversity, Equity, and Inclusion (DEI) initiatives, such as Employee Networks and a Global DEI Council, create a sense of belonging for all employees. Amex also prioritizes work-life balance through flexible work arrangements, wellness programs, and financial well-being support. With a dedicated Employee Relations Team to resolve conflicts and employee recognition programs that celebrate contributions, American Express creates a thriving, inclusive work environment where employees feel heard and appreciated, strengthening their commitment to the company.

## Strategy 2: Combat Retention Head-On

Employee retention programs focus on addressing turnover before it becomes a bigger issue. These programs often bring together employees from different departments to collaborate on retention strategies. For example, an early warning system might alert leadership to potential departures, enabling proactive engagement to boost morale.

## Real-World Example: Cleveland Clinic

At Cleveland Clinic, employee retention is a top priority, and the organization has implemented a proactive system to ensure staff are supported and engaged. Using predictive analytics, Cleveland Clinic monitors key indicators such as attendance, performance, and wellness data to identify employees at risk of burnout or turnover.

Through Employee Resource Groups (ERGs), staff can connect with supportive communities, while the Caregiver Experience Office collects real-time feedback to quickly address concerns. The clinic also conducts stay interviews to gauge job satisfaction and career aspirations, offering personalized support and growth opportunities.

Additionally, robust wellness programs that focus on mental health and burnout prevention help reduce stress in the high-pressure healthcare environment. This comprehensive approach allows Cleveland Clinic to address potential issues early, fostering a supportive culture where employees feel valued and are more likely to stay long-term.

## Strategy 3: Lean on Employee Assistance Programs (EAPs) for Support

EAPs offer support when personal challenges arise, and they're often underutilized. During tough times, employees may need confidential counseling, financial advice, or even wellness programs. Encouraging the use of EAPs not only helps employees bounce back but can also increase loyalty to the organization. Your organization could consider these incentives to boast about during recruitment, which can increase early interest in an organization from the start, and lead to them likely using the benefit once employed if they are aware that it exists.

## Real-World Example: The American Red Cross

At The American Red Cross, employees working in high-stress and emotionally challenging environments are supported by a comprehensive Employee Assistance Program (EAP) tailored to their unique needs. From the moment an employee joins, they have access to confidential mental health counseling, with specialized trauma support for those on the front lines of disaster response. The EAP offers real-time crisis counseling during critical incidents and ongoing support for work-related stress.

Employees can also take advantage of financial and legal assistance, with resources to help manage personal challenges like budgeting, retirement planning, or family legal issues. Additionally, the program offers childcare and eldercare support, making it easier for employees to balance their demanding roles with family responsibilities. Through peer support networks, wellness programs, and flexible work arrangements, the American Red Cross ensures its employees are well-cared for, fostering resilience and well-being even in the most challenging times.

## Strategy 4: Create Employee Resource Groups (ERGs)

ERGs provide a safe space for employees with shared backgrounds or experiences, such as disability, gender, race, or sexual orientation. These groups foster a sense of belonging and can be a powerful retention tool, especially for employees from diverse backgrounds. Organizations typically allow this type of experience to be self-formed, where they do not initiate for colleagues to connect based on these diverse elements, but they promote and offer the opportunity for employees to do so.

## Real-World Example: U.S. Department of Veterans Affairs (VA)

At the VA, ERGs play a pivotal role in fostering a diverse and inclusive workplace. These groups, such as VA Pride for LGBTQ+ employees, VALOR for veterans, and the Federal Employees with Disabilities (FED) Group, provide crucial support in areas like mentorship, career development, and advocacy. Through these ERGs, employees gain access to networking events, leadership development programs, and community-building activities that promote cultural awareness and professional growth.

The groups also work closely with senior leadership to shape inclusive policies, ensuring that the voices of underrepresented employees are heard. By advocating for work-life balance, flexibility, and accessibility, the VA's ERGs help create a workplace where all employees can thrive, contributing to a more supportive and dynamic organizational culture.

## Strategy 5: Get to Know Your Employees

Whether through staff meetings, picnics, or retreats, informal opportunities for connection help build stronger relationships. Leaders are encouraged to attend these events to interact with employees in a more relaxed setting, while team-building activities like happy hours or scavenger hunts can boost team dynamics and morale. Your organization could capitalize on these fun-filled outlets to increase retention by gaining an understanding of your employees' personalities, know what they enjoy, and encourage time for these occasional engagements.

## Real-World Example: Habitat for Humanity

At Habitat for Humanity, employee retreats are designed to foster connection, growth, and a deep sense of purpose. During these retreats, staff members come together to participate in hands-on home-building projects, which directly align with the organization's mission of providing affordable housing. These activities help employees reconnect with the core values of Habitat for Humanity while working side by side in a collaborative environment.

The retreats also feature leadership workshops and personal development sessions aimed at improving communication and teamwork, as well as strategic planning discussions that allow employees to reflect on past successes and plan future initiatives. To promote well-being, the retreat includes activities like yoga and mindfulness, helping staff relax and recharge. By combining mission-driven activities with personal and professional development, Habitat for Humanity's retreats leave employees feeling inspired, motivated, and reconnected to their impactful work.

## Addressing Challenges: Cultivating a Supportive Work Environment

As a leader, creating a supportive work environment is crucial for your organization's success, especially in today's diverse and often remote workplace. To tackle this challenge, focus on consistent and meaningful engagement with your team. Implement regular check-ins, ensure purpose-driven interactions, and balance your communication methods. Remember, employees who have regular meetings with their managers are three times more likely to be engaged. In the virtual workspace, bridge the digital divide by creating virtual water coolers, encouraging a video-first culture, and establishing clear communication protocols. Don't underestimate the power of virtual team building - even short social interactions before meetings can significantly improve team performance.

To truly support your employees, you need to know them. Leverage personality insights through comprehensive assessments and tailor your management approach accordingly. Assign tasks that align with your team members' natural strengths - this can increase productivity by up to 21%. Provide multiple avenues for support and engagement, including robust Employee Assistance Programs, structured mentorship programs, and diverse ERGs. Don't forget about mental health support - 86% of employees treated for depression report improved work performance. Cultivate a culture of psychological safety by creating open feedback channels, celebrating diverse perspectives, and modeling vulnerability as a leader.

Lastly, focus on personalized growth and development. Co-create individual development plans with each employee, implement skill-sharing platforms, and encourage participation in cross-functional projects. Remember, creating a supportive work environment is an ongoing commitment, not a one-time achievement. Consistently adapt and refine your approaches based on employee feedback and changing workplace dynamics.

## Conclusion & Key Takeaways

Relationships are the foundation of a healthy and productive work environment. They shape organizational culture and significantly influence employee retention. By understanding and nurturing relationships within your team, you create a supportive, inclusive atmosphere where individuals can thrive. The strategies outlined in this chapter highlight the importance of fostering engagement, creating psychological safety, and aligning tasks with employees' strengths to boost productivity and job satisfaction.

## Takeaways

1. **Meaningful workplace relationships** improve loyalty, reduce turnover, and create a stronger sense of connection among employees, leading to higher retention rates.

2. **Personality assessments** like the Big Five and Myers-Briggs help managers tailor their leadership approach, enhancing team dynamics and individual performance by leveraging unique strengths.

3. **Employee engagement** through both formal and informal interactions, such as virtual water coolers or team-building

events, is essential in maintaining strong connections, particularly in hybrid and remote work environments.

4. **Employee Assistance Programs (EAPs) and Employee Resource Groups (ERGs)** are valuable yet often underutilized tools that can support well-being and foster a sense of belonging, improving overall workplace culture.

5. **Psychological safety** is critical in creating a space where employees feel comfortable sharing feedback and diverse perspectives. Leaders should model vulnerability to cultivate trust within teams.

6. **Personalized growth and development plans** not only help employees feel valued but also align their strengths with organizational goals, increasing both engagement and productivity.

**Now it's time to take action!**

1. Implement a comprehensive relationship-building program: Start by conducting a company-wide assessment to understand the current state of workplace relationships. Based on the results, develop a multi-faceted program that includes regular team-building activities, mentorship opportunities, and cross-departmental collaboration initiatives. Ensure that these activities cater to both in-person and remote employees, fostering connections across all work environments.

2. Enhance your leadership development strategy: Invest in training programs that help managers understand and leverage personality assessments like the Big Five or

3. Myers-Briggs. This will enable them to tailor their leadership approach to individual team members, improving communication and overall team dynamics. Additionally, incorporate modules on creating psychological safety and fostering inclusive environments to build stronger, more resilient teams.

4. Revitalize your Employee Assistance Programs (EAPs) and Employee Resource Groups (ERGs): Conduct a thorough review of your existing EAPs and ERGs to identify areas for improvement. Increase awareness of these programs through targeted communication campaigns, highlighting their benefits and success stories. Encourage employee participation by allocating time and resources for these initiatives, and consider creating new ERGs based on employee feedback to ensure they meet the diverse needs of your workforce.

## Resources

Relationships in the workplace as the foundation for organizational support of employees is a commonly researched area. To learn more about how to implement strategies in your work settings and to explore tools for employees, check out a few of the resources listed below:

## Books:

1. <u>Meaningful Alignment: Mastering Emotionally Intelligent Interactions at Work and in Life</u> by Susan Steinbrecher, Robert Schaefer, and Joanne Moyle. This

*Motivated to Stay*

book provides practical strategies for developing emotional intelligence to improve workplace relationships and personal interactions.

2. <u>Relationships 101</u> by John C. Maxwell: Maxwell offers concise, foundational principles for building and maintaining strong relationships in both professional and personal contexts.

3. <u>How to Work with (Almost) Anyone</u> by Michael Bungay Stanier: Stanier presents a framework of five key questions to help readers build better working relationships through intentional conversations and mutual understanding.

## Articles:

1. <u>Great Teams Are About Personalities, Not Just Skills</u> by Dave Winsborough and Tomas Chamorro-Premuzic

2. <u>The Importance of Positive Relationships in the Workplace</u> by Elaine Houston

3. <u>The Power of Healthy Relationships at Work</u> by Emma Seppala and Nicole K. McNichols

## Assessments for Employees and Teams:

1. <u>CliftonStrengths Assessment</u>

2. <u>The Myers-Briggs Type Indicator (MBTI)</u>

3. <u>DISC Test</u>

## Sample Reflection Questions

1. What are the key strategies mentioned for fostering strong workplace relationships, and how can you apply them in your organization?

2. How does understanding individual personalities, using tools like the Big Five or Myers-Briggs, help improve team dynamics and productivity in your work environment?

3. Reflect on your current team. Are there opportunities to improve engagement through virtual water coolers, video-first culture, or informal team-building activities?

4. How can you better promote underutilized resources like Employee Assistance Programs (EAPs) or Employee Resource Groups (ERGs) within your organization?

5. What steps can you take to create a culture of psychological safety where employees feel comfortable providing feedback and sharing diverse perspectives?

6. How can co-creating individualized development plans enhance your team's growth and retention?

7. Think about a time when you felt especially supported in the workplace. What contributed to that feeling, and how can you replicate it for others in your team?

8. How do you currently foster mentorship and support within your organization, and how can these efforts be improved?

9. What role does vulnerability play in leadership, and how can modeling vulnerability improve trust and relationships in your team?

10. In what ways can you adapt your employee engagement strategies to better meet the needs of remote or hybrid teams?

# CHAPTER 9

# Pillar 8 - Onboarding & Exit Strategies: A Smooth Start & Valuable End

———————— ✦ ————————

The way new hires are onboarded into an organization can be a strong indicator of their long-term success and retention. A positive recruitment process that seamlessly transitions into a smooth onboarding experience significantly increases the chances of a happy, well-prepared new hire who is set up for success from the start. And as long as that consistency continues throughout their role, you're setting them up for long-term retention, as we've touched on in previous chapters.

For both employers and new hires, the recruitment process takes time and effort. So, when that new hire begins preparing for their new role, a blend of excitement, anxiety, and high expectations tends to follow. As a leader, you have a unique opportunity to influence and manage these emotions, ensuring your new hires feel supported right from the start—ultimately increasing the likelihood they'll stay for the long haul. This chapter will take you through the key stages of preboarding, onboarding, and exit strategies, highlighting why they're so critical to the employee experience.

## Case Study: Ritz-Carlton's Gold Standards - Setting the Bar for Luxury Onboarding

The Ritz-Carlton Hotel Company has set a new standard in the hospitality industry with its exceptional onboarding process, known as the "Gold Standards." This comprehensive approach begins even before an employee's first day and extends well into their tenure with the company. From the personalized welcome package sent a week before start date to the 21-day reinforcement program, Ritz-Carlton ensures that new hires are fully immersed in the company's culture, values, and service standards. Key elements include the Three Steps of Service, daily line-ups, empowerment training, and cross-departmental exposure, all designed to create a deep understanding of the Ritz-Carlton legacy and operational interconnectedness.

The results of this meticulous onboarding process speak volumes about its effectiveness. Ritz-Carlton boasts an employee turnover rate of just 20% in an industry where 70% is common, demonstrating the power of their approach in fostering employee engagement and retention. Moreover, with 92% of guests reporting that their stay exceeds expectations and a 90% customer return rate, it's clear that this investment in employee onboarding translates directly into exceptional customer experiences. This case study illustrates how a well-structured, values-driven onboarding process can create a strong foundation for both employee satisfaction and business success, offering valuable lessons for organizations across all sectors.

## The Science Behind Employee Experiences

Recent studies show that career paths are increasingly non-linear, with millennials expecting frequent job changes and the World Economic Forum predicting a need for continuous reskilling. This shift challenges the traditional view of career stages and emphasizes the importance of ongoing development throughout one's professional life.

The link between job satisfaction and productivity is well-established, with research indicating that happy employees are significantly more productive and engaged teams show greater profitability. Today's ideal employment journey encompasses a holistic approach, from pre-boarding to exit experiences, focusing on continuous development, flexibility, purpose alignment, and wellness integration.

## The Cost of Neglect: A Wake-Up Call for Employers

As an employer, you're not just filling a position when you hire someone new - you're making an investment in your company's future. But here's the harsh reality: if you neglect the crucial processes of onboarding and offboarding, you're setting yourself up for a costly failure. Imagine losing a new hire within months because they weren't properly integrated, costing you up to 150% of their salary. Or picture a team of disengaged employees, sticking around but contributing far less than their potential, all because their introduction to your company fell flat. These aren't just hypothetical scenarios - they're the very real consequences of neglecting these critical stages of the employee lifecycle.

But the damage doesn't stop there. When you lose key talent due to poor onboarding, you're not just losing an employee - you're losing time, resources, and potentially your competitive edge. And if that weren't enough, a mishandled exit can tarnish your employer brand for years to come, making it harder to attract top talent in the future. The message is clear: investing in effective onboarding and exit strategies isn't just a nice-to-have - it's essential for your company's success and sustainability. Can you really afford to neglect these crucial processes?

## The Benefits of Improvement: Crafting a Lasting Positive Legacy

When you focus on creating an exceptional employee experience from hire to exit, you're not just improving retention - you're building a powerful legacy that can transform your organization. Imagine former employees speaking positively about their time with you, or even returning as "boomerang" hires. This positive reputation can be a game-changer in attracting top talent, with 78% of job seekers considering a company's reputation before applying. Companies like Salesforce, consistently ranked among the best places to work, demonstrate the power of prioritizing employee experience.

Moreover, engaged employees are significantly more productive, with strong onboarding processes improving new hire retention by up to 82%.

The benefits extend far beyond your current workforce. Effective offboarding ensures crucial institutional knowledge isn't lost when someone leaves, while alumni networks can lead to new business opportunities and valuable referrals. Happy employees create satisfied customers, with highly engaged staff helping companies outperform competitors by 147%. Inclusive and innovative workplace cultures foster adaptability and creativity, essential in today's fast-paced business world. All these elements contribute to long-term business performance, with engaged employees driving higher customer loyalty and revenue growth.

## Strategies for Improvement

1. Leverage preboarding

2. Outline onboarding as a journey

3. Craft the smooth exit

## Strategy 1: Leverage Preboarding

Preboarding is the period between when an offer is accepted and when the new hire starts. This phase is all about building excitement and connection. Beyond the typical paperwork and logistical details, consider personal touches like a welcome video from the CEO or a phone call from the hiring manager. Early engagement—like a "Day in the Life" video or a welcome portal with essential resources—helps bridge the gap between acceptance and start date, keeping new hires excited and informed.

Preboarding activities also allow organizations the opportunity to continue educating the new hire about their mission, vision, and values so that they are knowledgeable about the organization and connected to the culture early on. The assumption is that new hires would not be hearing this information for the first time, because a good recruitment strategy should incorporate educating new hires about these areas to determine alignment on values and scope out their fit. The main goal is that new hires would have consistent experiences from recruitment up to the day they start, where these key fundamental elements of the organization are addressed multiple times since they are closely connected with how an organization's culture is built.

## Real-World Example: Warby Parker

Warby Parker sets a gold standard for preboarding with their innovative approach to welcoming new hires. Their process begins with a thoughtful "Welcome Box" containing company swag, a pair of glasses, and a book that inspired the company's name. This tangible gesture is complemented by an online platform where new hires can explore company history, take quizzes about the mission, and enjoy a virtual office tour. The company maintains regular communication through manager and HR check-ins, provides role-specific online training, and invites new hires to join their internal social network. They even assign a small task related to their social mission, allowing new employees to make an impact before their official start date.

This comprehensive preboarding strategy has yielded impressive results for Warby Parker. New hires are ramping up faster, showing higher engagement levels, and demonstrating improved retention rates. The company's approach has also enhanced its employer brand, attracting more top-tier candidates. Warby Parker's example illustrates how a creative and thoughtful preboarding process can create a powerful first impression, making new hires feel valued and excited about their new role. It demonstrates that effective preboarding goes beyond paperwork and logistics, focusing instead on creating a welcoming, engaging experience that sets the stage for long-term employee satisfaction and success.

## Strategy 2: Outline Onboarding as a Journey

Onboarding isn't a one-time event. It's a journey that begins when the new hire accepts the role and continues throughout their early days on the job. A well-structured onboarding experience, with clear goals and personal touches, can make a huge difference. From orientation to socialization with peers and mentors, your focus should be on making new hires feel welcome and equipped to succeed.

Orientation should answer the critical question: "What's in it for me?" For example, a welcome kit, peer mentor program, or a site tour can help new hires settle in. But beyond that, clarity about job expectations, where to find resources, and who to go to for help will ease their transition and reduce those first-day jitters. Keep in mind, retention starts on Day 1, so it's important to get it right.

## Real-World Example: Etsy

Etsy, the e-commerce platform for handmade and vintage items, has revolutionized the onboarding process with their "Etsy School" program. This six-week journey begins with an intensive week-long orientation, immersing new hires in the company's unique culture and values through interactive workshops, leadership meetings, and hands-on experiences like creating their own Etsy shop. The program continues with a series of "classes" over the next five weeks, covering everything from the company's business model to its technology stack. For engineers, there's a special "Bootcamp" program involving a month-long rotation through different teams, working on real projects. To ensure a smooth social transition, each new hire is paired with an experienced "buddy" who guides them through their new work environment.

The results of this comprehensive approach are impressive, with Etsy seeing a 20% increase in employee engagement scores for new hires and a 15% jump in first-year employee retention rates. New hires are also reaching full productivity about 30% faster than before. Etsy's approach demonstrates that effective onboarding goes beyond mere orientation; it's about creating an immersive experience that helps new employees truly understand and connect with the company.

## Strategy 3: Craft the Smooth Exit

When an employee decides to move on, how they leave can be just as important as how they started. A smooth exit process—complete with knowledge transfer, organized handovers, and engaging exit interviews—can make all the difference. It's an opportunity to learn why they're leaving and gather feedback to improve the experience for future employees. Treat every exit as a revolving door; if done well, high-performing employees may one day return.

## Real-World Example: Duolingo

Duolingo, the popular language-learning app, has revolutionized the employee exit process with their "Duo Alumni" program. Instead of treating departures like a bad breakup, they've transformed them into positive transitions. The program begins with a comprehensive knowledge transfer process, where departing employees document their projects, share insights, and create video tutorials for their successors. This is followed by "exit conversations" - genuine discussions about the employee's experience, reasons for leaving, and ideas for company improvement. These conversations go beyond traditional exit interviews, demonstrating Duolingo's commitment to learning and growth even as employees depart.

The program's impact extends far beyond the exit process itself. Duolingo maintains connections with former employees through a dedicated LinkedIn group and regular newsletters, sharing company updates and job openings. This approach has yielded impressive results, with about 10% of new hires being "boomerang" employees. The alumni network has become a valuable source of referrals and partnerships, and Duolingo's Glassdoor ratings have improved significantly, with many positive reviews coming from former employees. By treating exits as transitions rather than endings, Duolingo has created a community that extends beyond its current workforce, effectively turning former employees into brand ambassadors. This innovative approach demonstrates that an employee's departure can be an opportunity for continued relationship-building and future collaboration, rather than a final goodbye.

## Addressing Challenges in Onboarding and Exit Processes

Implementing new onboarding and exit processes can present three main challenges: maintaining clarity and consistency, leveraging technology effectively, and handling conflicts. To overcome these hurdles, start by ensuring all team members are aligned on the processes through regular check-ins and clear documentation. Create a simple 'cheat sheet' to keep everyone on the same page, fostering a welcoming environment for new hires. Embrace technology as your ally in streamlining these processes. Utilize onboarding and exit platforms to automate tedious tasks, saving time and collecting valuable data to inform future improvements.

When conflicts arise, approach them with a detective's mindset: ask questions, listen actively, and seek to understand the root cause. Quick resolution is key to maintaining a positive work environment.

Remember, each interaction during these processes is an opportunity to demonstrate your company's values and leave a lasting impression. With clear communication, smart technology use, and effective conflict resolution, you can transform potential pitfalls into stepping stones for success, ensuring that every step of the employee journey—from the first day to the final farewell—is a positive experience.

## Conclusion & Key Takeaways

Building strong workplace relationships isn't just about creating a positive atmosphere—it's a strategic imperative that drives employee retention, engagement, and overall organizational success. These relationships, like the roots of a tree, are fundamental to an organization's stability and growth. By prioritizing meaningful connections, fostering inclusivity, and encouraging open communication, you can cultivate a culture where employees feel valued, motivated, and committed to your company's long-term goals.

## Takeaways

1. **Personalization Matters**: One-size-fits-all strategies don't work. Tailor your relationship-building efforts to suit individual employees' personalities and needs.

2. **Leverage Technology Effectively**: Use tools to facilitate communication and collaboration, especially in remote or

hybrid settings, but ensure they complement, not replace, human interaction.

3. **Foster Inclusivity**: Create a work culture where diversity is valued, and every employee feels a sense of belonging.

4. **Invest in Development**: Mentorship and career growth programs are crucial to fostering long-term relationships and improving retention.

5. **Encourage Open Communication**: Promote an environment where feedback is welcomed, and employees feel heard—this builds trust and stronger relationships.

6. **Recognition Strengthens Bonds**: Regularly recognizing and appreciating employees not only boosts morale but also reinforces their connection to the organization.

7. **Balance Formal and Informal Interactions**: While structured programs are important, don't underestimate the power of casual, spontaneous interactions in building workplace relationships.

The strength of workplace relationships directly impacts retention. By investing in them, you're creating a supportive, engaged, and productive workforce that is loyal and committed for the long term.

**It's time to take action!**

1. **Implement a comprehensive relationship-building program:** Start by conducting a company-wide assessment to understand the current state of workplace relationships. Use this data to develop a multi-faceted program that includes regular team-building activities, mentorship

opportunities, and cross-departmental collaboration initiatives. Ensure these activities cater to both in-person and remote employees, fostering connections across all work environments. For example, you could introduce a monthly "Coffee Roulette" where employees are randomly paired for virtual or in-person coffee chats, encouraging connections beyond immediate teams.

2. **Enhance your leadership development strategy:** Invest in training programs that help managers understand and leverage personality assessments like the Big Five or Myers-Briggs. This will enable them to tailor their leadership approach to individual team members, improving communication and overall team dynamics. Additionally, incorporate modules on creating psychological safety and fostering inclusive environments. For instance, you could implement a "Leadership Lab" series where managers practice scenarios that require adapting their communication style to different personality types and creating inclusive team environments.

3. **Revitalize your Employee Assistance Programs (EAPs) and Employee Resource Groups (ERGs):** Conduct a thorough review of your existing EAPs and ERGs to identify areas for improvement. Increase awareness of these programs through targeted communication campaigns, highlighting their benefits and success stories. Encourage employee participation by allocating time and resources for these initiatives, and consider creating new ERGs based on employee feedback. For example, you could launch a "ERG Spotlight" series in your company newsletter,

featuring different groups each month and showcasing how they contribute to the company culture and support employee well-being.

## Resources

There are countless ways to approach onboarding and exit strategies for your employee experiences. Below are resources to help you navigate and see what other organizations have done.

## Books:

1. <u>The First 90 Days: Proven Strategies for Getting Up to Speed Faster and Smarter, Updated and Expanded</u> by Michael D. Watkins

2. <u>Creative Onboarding Programs: Tools for Energizing Your Orientation Program</u> by Doris M. Sims

3. <u>The WOW Factor Workplace: How to Create a Best Place to Work Culture</u> by Deb Boelkes.

## Articles:

1. <u>12 Exit Interview Questions Every HR Professional Should Ask</u> by Andrew Peeling

2. <u>Making Exit Interviews Count</u> by Everett Spain and Boris Groysberg

3. <u>14 Onboarding Best Practices</u> by Kelly Main

## Sample Reflection Questions

1. How does your organization currently approach onboarding and exit processes? What improvements could you make to ensure these are positive, value-driven experiences?

2. What specific strategies have you used in the past to build strong workplace relationships? How effective were they?

3. How do personalization and inclusivity play a role in your relationship-building efforts with employees?

4. What technology tools does your organization use to foster connections, and how can they be better utilized without replacing genuine human interaction?

5. How can mentorship and career development opportunities be enhanced to strengthen relationships and boost retention?

6. What steps can you take to promote more open communication and build trust within your team?

7. In what ways do you balance formal programs and informal interactions to nurture workplace relationships? How can this balance be improved?

8. How do you recognize and appreciate your employees regularly? How does this impact your team's morale and relationships?

9. What role do workplace relationships play in your organization's overall culture, and how can you foster a sense of belonging and community?

10. How do you see strong workplace relationships influencing employee retention in your organization? What adjustments could be made to strengthen these relationships?

# FINAL THOUGHTS

# Charting Your Path to Retention Excellence

———————⚜———————

As we reach the end of our journey through *Motivated to Stay,* it's clear that retention is not just a human resources issue — it's a critical business imperative that impacts every aspect of your organization. Throughout this book, we've explored the eight pillars of the Retention100™ assessment, providing you with actionable strategies and real-world examples to transform your approach to employee retention.

**Let's take a moment to reflect on the key points we've covered:**

1. **Leadership and Culture:** Strong, empathetic leadership and a positive workplace culture are foundational to retention success.

2. **Compensation and Benefits:** Competitive pay and comprehensive benefits are essential, but they're just the starting point.

3. **Work-Life Balance:** Flexibility and respect for personal time are increasingly crucial for employee satisfaction and loyalty.

4. **Career Development:** Providing clear growth paths and learning opportunities keeps employees engaged and committed.

5. **Recognition and Rewards**: Regular, meaningful acknowledgment of employee contributions boosts morale and retention.

6. **Communication and Feedback:** Open, transparent communication fosters trust and helps address issues before they lead to turnover.

7. **Diversity and Inclusion**: Creating an inclusive environment where all employees feel valued is key to retention in today's diverse workforce.

8. **Employee Well-being**: Prioritizing physical and mental health supports overall job satisfaction and longevity.

Now that you've completed the Retention100™ assessment, you have a clear picture of your organization's strengths and areas for improvement. It's time to take action. Here are the next steps to implement your top strategies:

1. **Prioritize your focus areas**: Based on your assessment results, identify the 3-5 pillars where your organization needs the most improvement.

2. **Develop an action plan:** For each priority area, create a detailed plan with specific goals, timelines, and responsible parties.

3. **Engage your team**: Share your retention goals with your leadership team and employees. Their buy-in and input are crucial for success.

4. **Implement and monitor**: Put your plans into action and regularly track progress using the metrics we've discussed throughout the book.

5. **Adjust and refine**: Be prepared to adapt your strategies based on feedback and results. Retention is an ongoing process, not a one-time fix.

As you embark on this journey to improve retention, remember the profound impact it can have on your organization. Effective retention strategies don't just keep employees—they create a thriving workplace where people are motivated to do their best work. This leads to increased productivity, innovation, and customer satisfaction, ultimately driving your organization's success.

Consider the ripple effects of improved retention: reduced recruitment costs, preserved institutional knowledge, stronger team dynamics, and a more positive company reputation. These benefits compound over time, creating a virtuous cycle that attracts top talent and propels your organization forward.

The landscape of work is evolving rapidly, and organizations that prioritize retention will be best positioned to navigate these changes. By implementing the strategies outlined in this book and continually refining your approach based on your Retention100™ assessment, you're not just reducing turnover—you're building a resilient, engaged workforce that can adapt to whatever challenges the future may bring.

Remember, every step you take towards improving retention is an investment in your organization's future. The journey may be challenging at times, but the rewards—a loyal, productive, and passionate workforce—are well worth the effort.

As you close this book, we encourage you to see it not as the end of your retention journey, but as the beginning of a transformative process that will shape your organization for years to come. Your employees are your most valuable asset. By prioritizing their satisfaction, growth, and well-being, you're laying the foundation for sustainable success.

Now, armed with knowledge, strategies, and your personalized Retention100™ assessment results, it's time to take action. Your employees—and your organization's future—are counting on you. Let's make retention a cornerstone of your organizational strategy and build a workplace where people don't just stay, but thrive.

# EPILOGUE

# The Future of Retention

As we conclude our exploration of *Motivated to Stay*, it's crucial to look beyond the present and consider how future trends will shape employee retention in the years to come. The workplace is evolving rapidly, and organizations must be proactive in addressing these changes to remain competitive. The importance of retention strategies has never been clearer, with studies showing that replacing an employee can cost up to 200% of their annual salary. The costs go beyond financials, impacting team morale, productivity, and organizational culture.

## Technological Disruption and AI Integration

**Automation and Artificial Intelligence Impact on the Workforce**

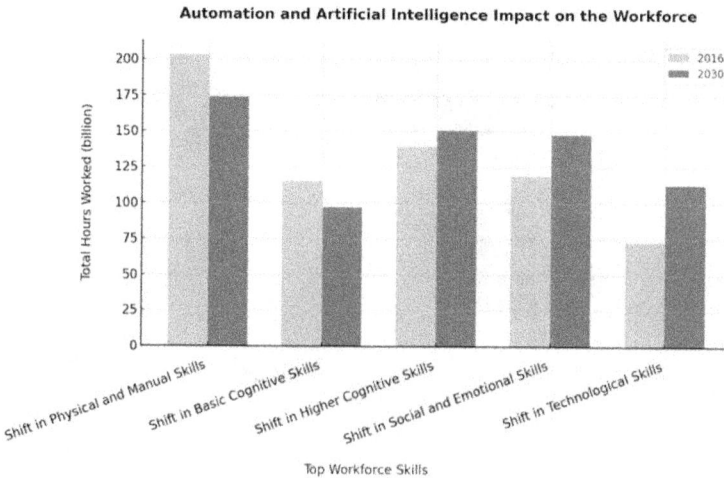

As technology advances, particularly in the areas of artificial intelligence (AI) and automation, the nature of work is fundamentally changing. A study by the McKinsey Global Institute predicts that by 2030, between 400 million and 800 million jobs could be displaced by automation, prompting organizations to invest heavily in upskilling and reskilling efforts. Employers who fail to provide development opportunities risk higher turnover as employees seek out organizations that offer career longevity in an increasingly automated world. Additionally, the integration of AI into HR functions, from recruitment to performance evaluations, will require new metrics for engagement and retention, focusing on personalization, adaptability, and fairness.

**Artificial Intelligence (AI) Impact Across the Workforce**

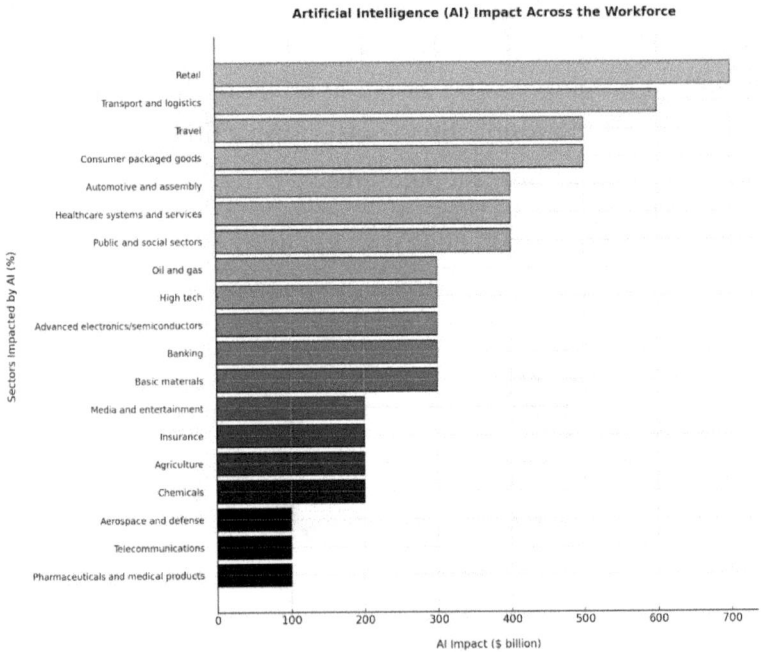

## Data-Driven Retention

In the future, retention strategies will become more data-driven, allowing organizations to predict turnover risk before it happens. Predictive analytics tools are already being used to assess employee sentiment, engagement levels, and even external factors that might influence turnover, such as labor market conditions or competitor activity.

Companies like IBM and Google have used AI-driven analytics to reduce turnover by up to 25%. As these tools become more refined, they will enable HR teams to tailor retention strategies to specific employee segments, offering more personalized career paths, rewards, and development opportunities.

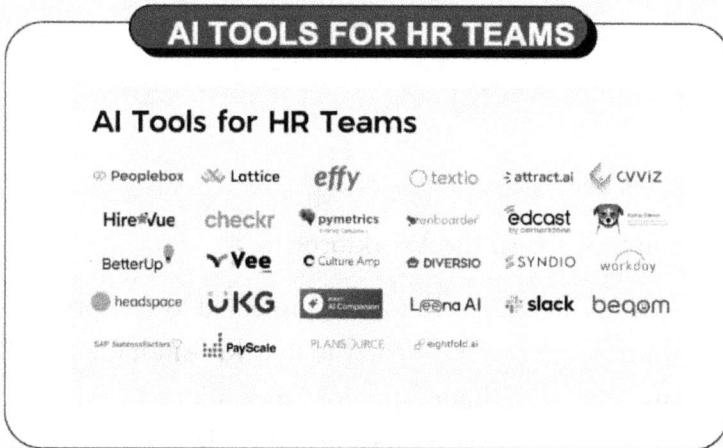

## The Rise of the Gig Economy and Portfolio Careers

The traditional career ladder is being replaced by more fluid career paths. According to a study by Intuit, by 2027, the gig economy is expected to grow to represent 60% of the workforce. This shift reflects employees' increasing desire for autonomy, flexibility, and purpose. As a result, retention strategies will need to evolve to accommodate workers who engage with organizations on a project or part-time basis. Companies that can offer gig workers benefits traditionally reserved for full-time employees, such as training, development, and wellness programs, will have a competitive edge in retaining top talent.

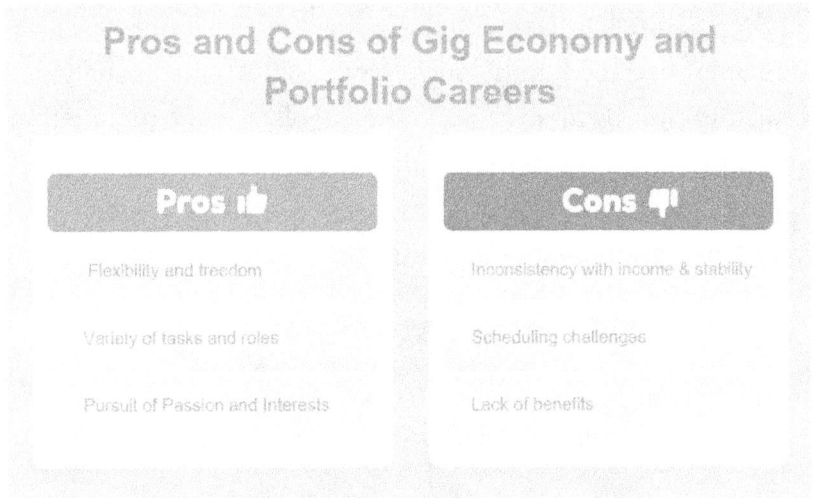

## Pros and Cons of Gig Economy and Portfolio Careers

| Pros 👍 | Cons 👎 |
|---|---|
| Flexibility and freedom | Inconsistency with income & stability |
| Variety of tasks and roles | Scheduling challenges |
| Pursuit of Passion and Interests | Lack of benefits |

## Generational Shifts in the Workforce

By 2025, Millennials and Gen Z are projected to comprise 75% of the global workforce, according to the Pew Research Center. These generations bring with them different expectations around work-life balance, purpose, and social responsibility. Research by Deloitte shows that 49% of Millennials and Gen Zs are willing to quit a job within two years if they feel their employer's values don't align with their own. To retain these workers, organizations must align with social causes, offer flexibility, and provide meaningful work that contributes to broader societal impact. Organizations that fail to adapt to these shifting values will struggle with engagement and retention.

**Gen Zs and Millennials Optimism for Addressing Societal Challenges
(Compared to the direction of their country)**

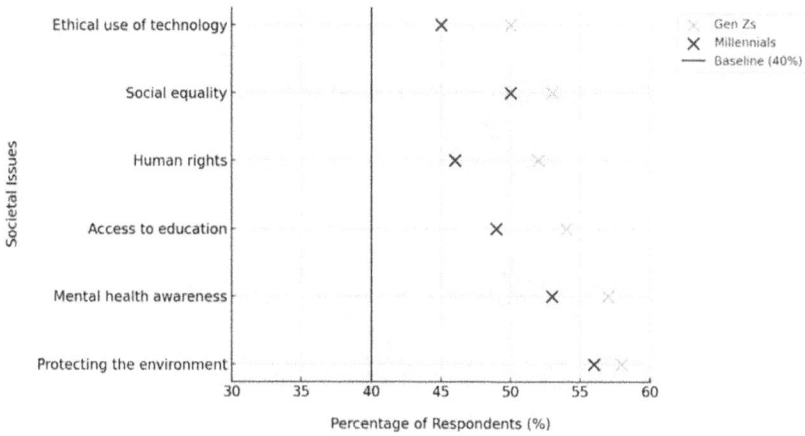

| Societal Issues | | |
|---|---|---|
| Ethical use of technology | X | Gen Zs |
| | | X Millennials |
| | | — Baseline (40%) |
| Social equality | X | |
| Human rights | X | |
| Access to education | X | |
| Mental health awareness | X | |
| Protecting the environment | X | |

Percentage of Respondents (%)
30   35   40   45   50   55   60

# Personalization of the Employee Experience

Just as customer experiences have become hyper-personalized, the future of retention will see the rise of personalized employee experiences. Employees increasingly expect their work environment, benefits, and career development opportunities to reflect their individual needs and preferences. According to Gartner, companies that adopt an individualized approach to employee engagement will see up to a 24% increase in retention. Future-forward organizations will use technology and employee feedback to customize learning opportunities, wellness programs, and flexible working arrangements that align with each employee's unique life and career stage.

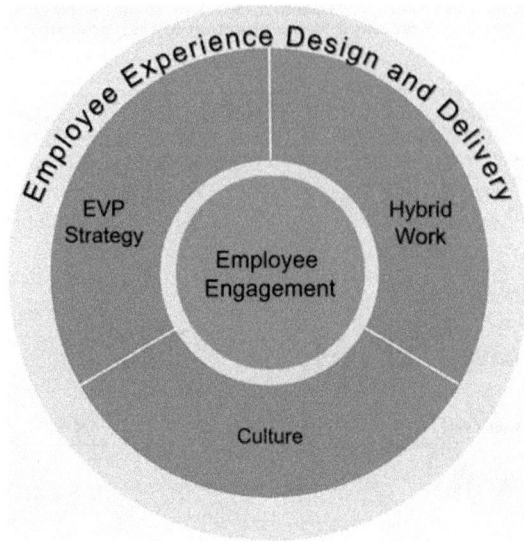

## Sustainability and Ethical Practices

With growing awareness around climate change and ethical business practices, employees are increasingly seeking employers that align with their values. A 2022 report by the Society for Human Resource Management (SHRM) found that 70% of employees would be more likely to stay with a company that has a strong sustainability agenda. As ESG (Environmental, Social, and Governance) becomes central to corporate strategy, future retention strategies will need to reflect how a company's purpose and sustainability initiatives resonate with its workforce. Organizations that can demonstrate meaningful contributions to social and environmental issues will not only attract top talent but retain them as loyal employees.

**Employee Willingness to Work for Employers with an ESG Strategy**

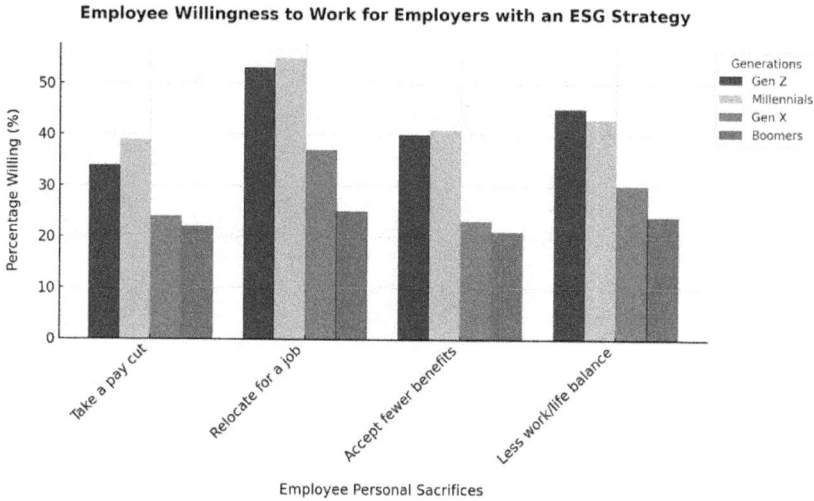

## Focusing on Well-Being and Mental Health for Retention

Companies often pressure workers to do more with less, which perpetuates the mental health crisis. The pandemic has permanently altered how employees view their relationship with work, with 80% of workers in a 2023 Gallup poll stating they would consider leaving a job that doesn't prioritize mental health. Future retention strategies will need to address holistic well-being—mental, physical, and emotional—by providing access to mental health resources, flexible working conditions, and fostering a culture of open communication. The workplace of the future will view well-being not as a perk but as a foundational pillar of retention.

**Negative Impacts of Work-Related Stress (NET)**

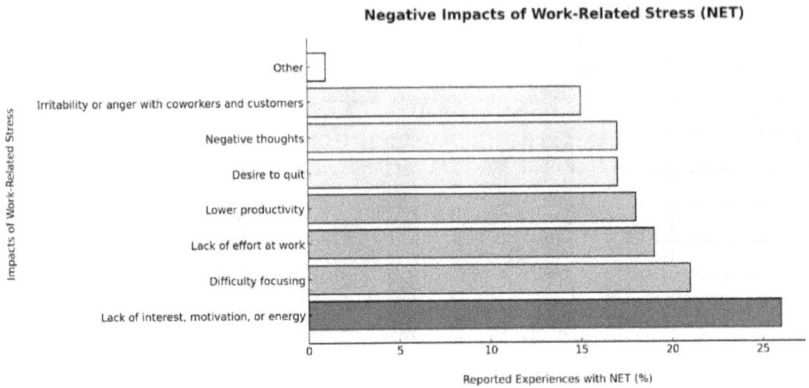

Reported Experiences with NET (%)

## The Role of DEI in Retention

Diversity, Equity, and Inclusion (DEI) initiatives are no longer optional; they are essential. A 2023 LinkedIn study found that 67% of job seekers consider a diverse workforce a major factor when evaluating job offers. As demographic shifts continue to diversify the global workforce, future retention efforts must prioritize creating an inclusive culture where employees of all backgrounds feel valued and supported.

Organizations that succeed in embedding DEI into their core values and everyday operations will have a significant advantage in attracting and retaining diverse talent.

**DIVERSITY**

- 60% of respondents said that diversity within their sales team contributed to their teams' success.
- Organizations in the top quartile for gender diversity have a +25% likelihood of financially outperforming their peers.
- Organizations in the top quartile for ethnic diversity have a +36% likelihood of financial outperformance.
- Diverse companies earn 2.5x higher cash flow per employee.
- Inclusive teams are over 35% more productive.
- Diverse teams make better decisions 87% of the time.

## Redefining Leadership for the Future Workforce

As employees seek purpose, flexibility, and empathy from their leaders, command-and-control leadership models will give way to more collaborative, coaching-oriented approaches. Studies show that employees with empathetic leaders are 50% less likely to burn out and are significantly more engaged at work. In the future, leaders will need to prioritize emotional intelligence, adaptability, and transparency to foster trust and loyalty, ensuring that employees feel connected to the company's mission and their individual role within it.

**EMPATHY IN ACTION**

- Leaders can express gratitude and appreciation for employees' effort/work.
- Discuss how the leader experienced a similar situation.
- Direct employees to a supportive assistance program.
- Develop a personal self-care program to maintain own well-being while effectively leading employees.

# Go Deeper

The authors of *Motivated to Stay* offer a variety of services to help your organization keep their best people. Our offerings include coaching, consulting, training, and keynote speaking. Whether you want to certify your L&D team, train your managers on leadership, or coach your executives, we have the solution. Contact us for more information.

# ONLINE
# CERTIFICATE
# PROGRAM

Motivated to Stay: 100 Strategies for
Keeping Your Best People

Instructor/Facilitator: The sessions will be
facilitated by William J. Rothwell, creator of
the Retention100TM.

**1** THREE 90-MINUTE MEETINGS

**2** ONLINE SESSIONS

**3** PRICE GUARANTEE

**SESSION 1:**
**UNDERSTANDING THE**
**COST AND CAUSES OF**
**TURNOVER**

**SESSION 2:**
**THE EIGHT PILLARS OF**
**THE RETENTION100™**

**SESSION 3:**
**CRAFTING AND**
**IMPLEMENTING A**
**RETENTION ACTION PLAN**

https://www.rothwellandassociates.com   info@RothwellAndAssociates.com

# Turnkey Retention Solutions

## COACHING

HELPING EXECUTIVES
RECOVER FROM
BURNOUT IN 90 DAYS

## CONSULTING

TRAIN THE TRAINER
LEADERSHIP TRAINING
TURNOVER
REDUCTION

## SPEAKING

THE ROLE OF
LEADERSHIP IN
RETENTION

## BOOK DR. SHARON GROSSMAN

Reclaim your energy
and elevate your
leadership.

Empower your team to
thrive and reduce
turnover.

Ignite your team's
motivation and
retention.

www.drsharongrossman.com | sharon@drsharongrossman.com

www.ingramcontent.com/pod-product-compliance
Lightning Source LLC
Chambersburg PA
CBHW061221220326
41599CB00025B/4711